The border is not just a wall. It's not just a line on a map. It's not any particular physical location. It's a power structure, a system of control. The border is everywhere that people live in fear of deportation, everywhere migrants are denied the rights accorded citizens, everywhere human beings are segregated into *included* and *excluded*.

The border does not divide one world from another. There is only one world, and the border is tearing it apart.

CrimethInc. Workers' Collective / 2017 / Salem, Oregon

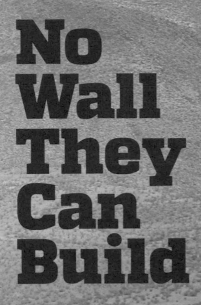

No Wall They Can Build

a guide to borders & migration across North America

Authored by an ex-desert-aid-worker

N©!2017 CrimethInc. ex-Workers' Collective
Abolish every border, including intellectual property rights

CrimethInc. Far East
PO Box 4671
Salem OR 97302
inquiries@crimethinc.com

A full-size electronic version of the diagram of the
North American border regime is available at
www.crimethinc.com/borders

You can obtain a print poster of the diagram and a great
deal of related material via www.crimethinc.com

*Printed in Canada by unionized printers
on 100% post-consumer recycled paper*

for everyone who didn't make it,
and for everyone who did

Si la visa universal se extiende
El día en que nacemos
Y caduca en la muerte
¿Por qué te persiguen *mojado*
Si el cónsul de los cielos
Ya te dio permiso?

If the universal visa is issued
On the day that we are born
And it expires with our death
Why do they persecute you, *wetback*
If the consul of the heavens
Already gave you permission?

-*"Mojado," Ricardo Arjona*

This book describes the US-Mexico border as I've experienced it since 2008. I wrote some sections of this text in 2011, which were distributed under the title Designed to Kill: Border Policy and How to Change It. I wrote the rest of it in 2016, in the months leading up to the US presidential elections. As of February 2017, it is too early to say if the Trump administration will fundamentally change the system that I describe here. It is possible that some of what I have to say will become outdated over the next few years.

For the time being, it seems inevitable that the suffering and death that I have witnessed on the border will continue to intensify under the new regime, and that the current authorities will persecute undocumented people even more ruthlessly than the former ones did. If so, I hope that this book will serve as a reminder that all was not well during the Clinton, Bush, or Obama years, either, and that the issues I address here will not be resolved by simply putting the right people back in charge. The question is not who should manage the border—it is how to abolish it.

But permit me to make my case.

non sum dignus

"They are coming! They are coming! ¡*Ya vienen!*"

It was clear and cold, and the Big Dipper had been revolving over our heads. José, María, and I were huddled together trying to stay warm. For the first time since I had met her María sounded panicked. Heavy boots were pounding towards us in the dark.

One of the agents threw some kind of lasso around us, and grabbed me by the neck.

"¡¿*Donde está tu grupo?! ¡¿Donde están los demás?!*"

"I'm going to remain silent. I'd like to speak to a lawyer." I tried to sound as calm as possible, but my voice probably broke.

I had been hiking well north of the border in southern California. I ran into José and María just before dark. They had been lost for days, and they were getting sicker by the hour. This was back during the Bush years. I didn't have a cell phone then. We were miles from my car, in a desolate place. I didn't know what to do. I decided to stay with them.

María's husband had abandoned her and her four children. She gave me to understand that she had been doing sex work in order to put food on the table. José had ridden the freight trains up to the border. He couldn't talk about it. I didn't know what exactly had happened to him during the trip.

I had a bad feeling that something was going to happen. A helicopter had circled over us earlier. On a cold night like that we lit up their infrared like a Christmas tree.

We were dead meat.

"Are you her husband? What are you doing out here? What the hell is going on! You're under arrest!"

"I'm going to remain silent. I'd like to speak to a lawyer."

They threw us into the van.

María had regained her composure. She put her arm around my shoulder. "*No te preocupes*," she told me, as we bounced along.

"Vamos a sobrevivir." Don't worry. We'll survive. José dropped his head, shook it back and forth, looked up at me, smiled, and dropped his head again.

They brought us to the Border Patrol detention facility. There were two hundred of us, sitting in rows under the lights, waiting to be taken in.

They had separated José and María from me. I could see them way over on the other side of the yard. I would never see José again. The man next to me spoke perfect English.

"I'm completely fucked, bro. My life is totally destroyed."

"I'm not doing so good either," I told him. "Where are you from?"

"Detroit," he said. "Motown! Lions roar! The 313, you know? My wife's there, my kids, everybody. This is the third time I've gotten caught trying to get back home. I'm going to jail for sure this time, and if they ever catch me again I don't even know what they'll do. I don't know how my wife is going to pay the bills, I don't know who's picking the kids up from school, I don't know anything."

"Me neither," I said.

"I wish I could put these motherfuckers in my shoes. I wish I could do them like they're doing me. I wish I could turn their lives upside down. I wish I could make somebody pay for this."

I looked over the sea of faces. "So do I."

They put eighty of us into a holding cell the size of a bedroom. We were piled on top of each other to the point that people had to take turns lying underneath the toilet. Each one of my arms and legs was stacked underneath or on on top of those of other people. One man was wearing a plastic hospital gown. The bandages on his left hand and bicep were soaked through with blood. The dogs had torn off his jacket and chewed up his arm.

Every once in a while the guards would pull me out of the cell for interrogation: "What do *you* care what happens to these people? Who do you work for? What were you *really* doing?"

"I'm going to remain silent. I'd like to speak to a lawyer."
Eventually they would give up and put me back in with the others.

The heat and stench and overcrowding got so bad that I thought that there would be a riot. People were starting to lose it. One of the older men tried to reason with one of the guards.

"*Officiál, por favór*, there are too many of us in here. The people are going to start fighting with each other. We would be easier to control if you would split us up into two cells."

"Fuck you, wetback. You shouldn't have gotten picked up on a weekend."

One of the younger men tried, also. "Sir, I take psych meds. They're with my stuff. I'm afraid I might start flipping out if I miss my dose. Can you see if you can find them?" .

"Yeah, yeah! You want your medication? Come here, I'll give you your medication!" They took him out of the cell, punched him in the face, and tazed him in front of all of us. "There's your fucking medication!"

Eventually, one of the older men stood up on the toilet and sang a *corrido*. One of the younger men followed suit, and then another, and then another, and against all odds the group kept its composure.

After three days of this, one of the guards opened up the door and pointed at me.

"You! U.S. citizen! Come with me! They're letting you go."

On our way out of the facility, the guard had to take a phone call. "Stay right here," he told me, and he left me alone, in front of the plate glass window of the women's holding cell. And there was María, sitting in the back. I waved frantically at her, and she walked up to the front of the cell.

I pointed at myself, and made the universal walking sign with my index and middle finger. She pointed at me, and then toward the exit down the hall. I nodded, and she nodded back. We looked at each other. She put her hand up to the glass, and

I put my hand up to hers. I made a fist with my other hand and tapped it three times over my heart. She made a fist and tapped three times back.

I could hardly keep it together. She wasn't going to Los Angeles, to send money home to her children and mom. She was going back to sex work in Mexicali. It just wasn't right.

Footsteps were coming down the hall. I broke eye contact at the last possible moment, turned around, and tried to look normal.

The guard rounded the corner. "Let's go, buddy. You're going home."

And I walked out the door behind him, blinking back tears, back into the sun.

Some years later, I moved to Arizona.

From 2008 until 2015, I worked in southern Arizona as part of a humanitarian aid organization named No More Deaths, acting in solidarity with migrants and refugees from Mexico and Central America who walk through the Sonoran Desert into the United States. Over more than twenty years, the government of the United States has channeled this stream of human movement into increasingly remote areas of its southern border, and many thousands of people have died from heat, cold, sickness, injuries, hunger, and thirst as a direct result. The mission of No More Deaths is to end this death and suffering in the borderlands.

No More Deaths was established in 2004, and people from all over the world and all walks of life have volunteered with us since then.* We've spent these years familiarizing ourselves

* No More Deaths is an open organization and our work is legal under American law. The American government has nonetheless arrested and attempted to prosecute our volunteers on various occasions. The July 2005 arrest of Daniel Strauss and Shanti Sellz was the most widely publicized case. As of this writing, all of these prosecutions have ultimately failed, and no one has ever been convicted of any crime in conjunction with our work in the desert.

with the Sonoran Desert. We find places to leave food and water along the trails that cross through it, look for migrants in distress, and provide medical care when we run into someone who needs it. We maintain a base camp in the desert year round where we can provide more extensive care. If a situation is bad enough, we can get an ambulance or helicopter to bring people to the hospital. We strive to act in accordance with travelers' wishes at all times, and we never call the Border Patrol on those who don't wish to turn themselves in. Our efforts have unquestionably helped to reduce the number of deaths on the Arizona border.

During the time that I worked in the desert, I was directly involved in many extraordinary situations and indirectly involved in many more. Some of the things I've seen have been truly heartwarming, and some of them have been deeply sad and wrong. I've seen people who were too weak to stand, too sick to hold down water, too badly hurt to continue, too scared to sleep, too sad for words, hopelessly lost, desperately hungry, literally dying of thirst, never going to be able to see their children again, vomiting blood, penniless in torn shoes two thousand miles from home, suffering from heat stroke, kidney damage, terrible blisters, wounds, hypothermia, post-traumatic stress, and just about every other tribulation you could possibly think of. I've been to places where people were robbed and raped and murdered; my friends have found bodies. In addition to bearing witness to the suffering of others I myself have fallen off of cliffs, torn my face open on barbed wire, run out of water, had guns pointed at me, been handcuffed, arrested, jailed, charged by bulls, circled by vultures, stalked by mountain lions, jumped over rattlesnakes, pulled pieces of cactus out of many different parts of my body with pliers, had to tear off my pants because they were full of fire ants, gotten gray hairs, and in general poured no small amount of my own sweat, blood, and tears into the thirsty desert. I have been humbled countless times by the incredible selflessness and courage of the people that I met there, and I have been driven nearly out of my head with rage at the heartless economic and political system that drives

people to such lengths in order to provide for their families. I met thousands of people like José and María, each with a unique story to tell but at least one thing in common: to the people who write border policy their lives hold no value, and their deaths bring no consequences.

Doing this work has given me a great deal of opportunity to observe how the border is managed on a day-to-day basis, and hopefully some insight into the functions it performs within global capitalism—the real objectives it serves. I've been positioned on one of the frontlines of global migration over an extended period of time, a vantage point shared by relatively few

This is how I see it:

North America comprises a single economy, which is divided by two major borders. One runs between the United States and Mexico, the other between Mexico and Guatemala.* Many people are compelled to migrate across these borders by pressures largely beyond their control. The objective of both American and Mexican border policy is not to stop this migration, but to manage and control it, to the benefit of identifiable sectors of both societies, and with the deaths of thousands of people as the predictable and intended result. Ultimately, immigration controls in this part of the world amount to a form of systematic segregation, in which the movements and civil rights of certain people are curtailed due to place of birth.

In other words, apartheid.

What's more, the same two borders that divide North America circumscribe the entire globe, for basically the same reasons and with basically the same results. They separate core states from buffer states, and buffer states from peripheral states. Just as North America comprises a single economy, there is only one world economy: it siphons resources through the marketplace

---

* For the purposes of this book, the US/Canada border is less important than the two southern borders. That being said, the Canadian immigration system is distinct from that of the United States; I'll leave the analysis to those who have experience with it. See *Undoing Border Imperialism* by Harsha Walia, for example.

"Charity, vertical, humiliates. Solidarity, horizontal, helps."

– Eduardo Galeano

from the periphery to the core.* Millions if not billions of human beings are either fungible or superfluous in this global economy, and these borders exist to regulate their movements: to keep these people in their place.

I believe that both basic decency and common sense dictate that citizens of the global north take concrete steps to undermine this global caste system, and to reintegrate ourselves with the rest of humanity. First, because it's the right thing to do. Also, because otherwise the situation will become so untenable that our own safety and survival will eventually be at stake. One place to start is on the border. There are many others places to begin.

This book is a product of the seven years that my friends and I spent in the desert, trying to find our way. It is a synthesis of countless conversations, interactions, and experiences that I shared with thousands of people: migrants, refugees, and undocumented people; people involved with human trafficking, drug smuggling, and law enforcement; my co-workers and fellow volunteers with No More Deaths; and people that I spent time with while living, working, traveling, and participating in social movements throughout Mexico and Central America. The conclusions I've come to are my own. I don't speak for the organization No More Deaths, or for anyone other than myself.

I think that most of what I have to say won't be news to many undocumented people, or to many people who live in Mexico or Central America. I'll take responsibility for anything that doesn't ring true. I'm writing mostly for readers with first-world citizenship

* I am paraphrasing Immanuel Wallerstein's world-systems analysis, although I arrived at similar conclusions on the basis of my experience in the desert before I discovered his work.

who are interested in understanding the dynamics of migration in North America, and especially for those working in the interests of migrants and refugees and for a world without borders. I hope that some of what I've seen can be useful toward that end.

I offer these words as ammunition to anyone who cares to intervene when other people are treated like pieces of meat.

"It's good that you keep the bones here," Jesús told me. We were standing in front of a large pile of bones, mostly deer and cow, that our volunteers had collected from the desert. "The animals suffer from hunger and thirst as we do. They are hunted as we are. They die alone as we do, and nobody knows or cares. It's good that they should be remembered also."

Jesús was working at a muffler shop in Bakersfield when he got deported. His wife and children were waiting for him there; they had been waiting for six months while he was stuck back in Michoacán. When he found our camp he had been walking through the desert for six days, alone and half-mad from dehydration and exposure.

His shoulder-length black hair was tied into a neat ponytail. He was wearing a weather-beaten denim jacket, faded blue jeans, a handsome belt buckle, a simple necklace, and a well-fitted black T-shirt from a Southern California motorcycle club. Even after such a terrifying ordeal, there was no denying that the man had style.

"They treat us like animals," he said.

Jesús is home now, welding mufflers and raising his children. Before he walked out of our camp and back into the desert he found a gigantic heart-shaped piece of driftwood in the *arroyo*, painted it blood red, and placed it on a waist-high pedestal of rocks he painted white.

"This is our heart," he told me. "The heart of the people, all of us, of everyone who walks here, of everyone who works here, of everyone who died here, of the cows and the deer and the rabbits, too. Maybe some day things will be different. I'll come back down here to visit and we'll all sit around this thing and tell stories about everything that happened."

May we live to see the day.

"Benedicto: May your trails be crooked, winding, lonesome, dangerous, leading to the most amazing view."
– Edward Abbey

Defining Terms

Absent any other qualifier, **the border** refers to the border between Mexico and the United States.

The desert refers to the part of the border in the Sonoran Desert of southern Arizona where I worked, mostly between Sasabe and Nogales.

The construction **migrants and refugees** refers to people without American citizenship who cross the border in order to live and work in the United States, with or without the authorization or documents required under American immigration regulations. I'll sometimes collapse this to "migrants" or "travelers." I make no distinction between "migrants" crossing the border for "economic" reasons and "refugees" crossing the border to "flee violence or persecution." In my experience, these are arbitrary categories, and most people's motivations are a combination of both. In many parts of the world, it's difficult to distinguish between poverty and "violence or persecution" in the first place.

However, "refugee" does have a definition under both American and international law. Many of the people who cross the border fall within this definition, and the American government has a legal obligation to treat them accordingly. The American government rarely meets this obligation, and has a vested interest in defining all such people as migrants. Because of this, I believe it's important to bring the term "refugee" into wider use in the United States to refer to people who cross the border, despite the fact that it doesn't necessarily describe every person. There are of course migrants and refugees from all over the world who enter the United States by other means than crossing the border, but that is outside the scope of this work.

Irregular migration refers to migration that takes place outside the regulatory norms of the sending, transit, or receiving countries.

Undocumented people refers to people who are inside of the United States or Mexico without the authorization or documents required under American or Mexican immigration regulations. Obviously these people possess documents, but no alternative phrase to describe the situation is in common use.

Solidarity worker refers to people (such as myself for seven years) who ascribe to radical politics, and whose political activity is oriented around the needs of others, in this case of migrants and refugees. This is not a common construction, but for many reasons I dislike the term "activist," and strongly dislike the less common alternative "ally." Neither term accurately describes our role on the border or in society at large.

The nearly perfect phrase "desert aid worker" is a neologism in constant use inside of No More Deaths, but unknown anywhere else. I aim to convey its spirit and broaden its scope, while still highlighting the fact that people such as myself are also subject to the pressures of capitalism.

I will sometimes use "**American**" as an adjective to refer to things pertaining to the United States. This usage is of course both geographically inaccurate and linguistically imperialist. However, as no alternative adjective (comparable to the Spanish *estadounidense*) exists in Standard "American" English, there is sometimes no way to avoid it.

From South to North

Start off anywhere . . .

The Aftermath

It's best to tell the hardest truth first.

Like the rest of the Western Hemisphere, the land that is currently called the United States of America, Mexico, Guatemala, El Salvador, and Honduras was stolen from its original inhabitants by European colonists through a well-documented orgy of bloodshed, treachery, and genocide of proportions so epic that they are arguably unprecedented in the thousands of often gruesome years of human history preceding them and unsurpassed in the hardly tranquil ones that followed. In progress for over five hundred years, this monstrous crime has never been atoned for in any meaningful way. It is still being perpetrated to this day.

Everybody knows this, but nobody really likes to think too much about what it means. What it means is this: unless you're honest enough to admit that you think that might makes right as long as you're on the winning side, you have to acknowledge that the federal, local, and state governments of these countries—including all their agencies such as Border Patrol, Customs and Border Protection, and Immigration and Customs Enforcement—are illegitimate institutions with no claim to legitimate authority over the territory they currently govern.

It's important to start by framing the matter thus. Who are these people that claim to have jurisdiction over native land? What right do they have to be telling anybody where to go and when? If anyone has a right to decide who can and cannot pass through North America, it's the people whose ancestors have inhabited that land since time immemorial, not the descendants or institutions of the ones who colonized it. Most so-called illegal immigrants have a more defensible claim to the continent they're traversing than most of the hypocrites who condemn and pursue them.

Furthermore, much of the wealth of the United States, like that of much of the rest of the Western Hemisphere, was accumulated through the greatest mass kidnapping and wage theft ever perpetrated in human history: the Atlantic slave trade and

> ## "The United States is not *at* war.
> ## The United States *is* war."
> *– Sora Han*

Southern plantation system. Once again, this monstrous crime has never been atoned for, and its impacts continue to be felt to this day.

Again—who is to say that these latest immigrants don't also deserve a piece of the pie? How many of the upstanding citizens clamoring for a wall have slave owners in their family trees? Not all, but plenty. I do. Are they willing to board airplanes and deport themselves back to Europe without delay? At least the people now crossing the border to better their station in life are willing to do the work themselves, rather than enslaving others to do it for them.

For over 500 years, the central narrative of the Western Hemisphere has been the ongoing story of slavery and colonization—the theft of lives, labor, and land. The aftermath of this process shapes everything that has followed. It's impossible to understand North America without putting this front and center.

There is a counter-narrative, too, just as old and strong, made up of countless stories of courage and resistance. I'll be telling some of those here as well.

One day, my colleague and I drove way out into the middle of nowhere to drop water in the desert. Four days later, it was time to check on it. On our way out to the spot, we saw a man sitting by the side of the little dirt road. He had a ripped up piece of blanket tied around one knee. "How are you doing?" I asked him.

"Badly," he answered. "Look at this." He pulled up his pant leg to reveal a black, swollen, thoroughly broken ankle.

"That's bad," I said. "You need to go to the hospital."

"Yes," he said. "Look at this." He pulled his shirt aside.

"OH *SHIT*!" my colleague and I shouted in unison, unprofessionally. He had a large open chest wound, bloody, half scabbed over and oozing pus. "You need to go to the hospital right *NOW*! What happened?"

"Four nights ago, I was walking with three other men through those mountains over there. I took a blind fall, ten or twelve feet over a cliff. I broke my ankle and sliced my chest open on a rock. They carried me down from there all through the night. In the morning we saw you drive by, but we were still too high, we couldn't get to the road in time. When we got here they left and said they were going to find help. I haven't seen them or anybody else since then."

"You've been here four days?" It had been well over a hundred degrees every day. "Have you had any food or water?"

"Food, no. A couple times a day I crawled over to that pond. I didn't want to get very far from the road in case someone drove by."

There was a dried up cattle pond a hundred yards from the road, at best an inch deep, mostly manure and sludge. There were about a dozen sets of drag marks where he had crawled between the pond and the road. We drove him to the ambulance. He was remarkably stoic about everything. I asked him if the bumpy road was hurting his ankle.

"No."

"Your chest?"

"No."

"You didn't get sick from the bad water?" I was sure that he would have died if he had.

"No. Just call my wife in Dallas and tell her I'm alive." I did. The ambulance took him to the hospital and I never heard from him again.

The Travelers

The vast majority of the people who cross the border are citizens of either Mexico* or the "Northern Triangle" of Central America: Guatemala, El Salvador, and Honduras. There are some exceptions; while working in the desert, I met a few people from Belize, Nicaragua, and Peru, and more than a few from Ecuador, but far more from Mexico and the Northern Triangle.†

What drives citizens of these countries across the border?

Most people in the world, all other things being equal, prefer to live wherever their immediate families live. However, millions of people are pushed and pulled between Mexico, the Northern Triangle, and the United States by a combination of powerful forces. Most parts of this cycle cannot solely be defined as a "push" or "pull" factor, but are both at once.

Taken individually, every story is different. Taken as a whole, nearly all the stories I've heard share one of three common themes. Over and over, I met people who said they were crossing the border because they had been deported and were returning home, because they were fleeing violence and poverty to the south, or because they could make a better living in the north. Often, it was a combination of all three. The particulars vary endlessly, but the pattern holds.

To state the obvious: migrants and refugees are possessed of agency and free will like everyone else. Generally speaking, people choose to do whatever they think is best from the options they have available.

So the first of the factors pulling people north and pushing people south is that the American government deports hundreds

* Most commonly, from the southern states of Oaxaca, Guerrero, Michoacán, Veracruz, and Chiapas.

† This is why I refer to the Northern Triangle rather than Central America: far fewer Nicaraguans, Belizeans, Costa Ricans, and Panamanians go to the United States to work, and far fewer of those who do so cross the border in order to get there.

of thousands of people to Mexico and the Northern Triangle every year. Many of the deportees' immediate families live in the United States, and many deportees have homes, jobs, and cars here as well. Regardless of citizenship, these are not people who live in Mexico or the Northern Triangle—they are people who live in the United States. Many have lived here for years and even decades. One of the most common reasons to cross the border into the United States is simply to return home.

Another factor that pushes people north is the widespread instability and violence throughout much of Mexico and the Northern Triangle. Many people cross the border primarily to get away from this. I'll explore what this looks like and why this is the case in the next section.

The last of the three primary factors that push and pull people north over the border is the wage and cost of living differential between the United States, Mexico, and the Northern Triangle—what Greek economist Arghiri Emmanuel refers to as "unequal exchange."

In absolute terms, the cost of living is somewhat lower in Mexico than in the United States, and lower still in the Northern Triangle. However, wages for comparable work are, to a disproportionate degree, much lower in Mexico than in the United States, and very much lower still in the Northern Triangle. For example, as of 2016, the federal minimum wage in the United States is $7.25 an hour, with much unskilled to semi-skilled labor paying around $10-15 dollars an hour. In Guatemala, a typical wage for the same labor could be anywhere from $0.35 to $1.50 an hour, with many people working precariously in the informal sector and guaranteed no earnings at all.

This holds true across the wage spectrum. Regardless of whether we are talking about bricklaying or open-heart surgery, the value of an hour's work will be much lower if performed in Mexico (or elsewhere in the global south) than if the same labor were performed in the United States (or elsewhere in the global north), and lower still if performed in the Northern Triangle (or elsewhere in the "deep south").

Furthermore, most imported goods are at least as expensive in Mexico as in the United States, and usually more so; they are usually more expensive still in the Northern Triangle. This goes for nearly anything exported from the United States or elsewhere in the global north and imported into Mexico, the Northern Triangle, or elsewhere in the global south—food, construction materials, automobiles, electronics, books, medicines, and so on. A used car, for instance, will invariably increase in value when it crosses the border from the United States to Mexico, and again when it leaves Mexico and enters Guatemala. Many Mexicans from border cities will buy groceries at the Safeway on the American side, if they have the papers to do so. Processed food is usually cheaper there. Textbooks can cost twice as much in Guatemala as in the United States.

Many Americans who have traveled across the border will have the impression that things are cheaper in Mexico—dental care is the most well known example. Not exactly. *Services* such as dental care are cheaper in Mexico. This makes sense; the cost of services reflects the value of wages. *Goods* are likely to be comparably priced if they are manufactured in Mexico, and more expensive if they are not.*

What's more, this applies to most goods manufactured in other parts of the global south and exported to Mexico or the Northern Triangle. A pair of jeans made in Bangladesh or a cell phone made in China will not be any cheaper at a Wal-Mart in Tuxtla Gutiérrez or Tegucigalpa than a Wal-Mart in Tulsa, and may well be more expensive.

So, while the *absolute* cost of living is lower in Mexico than in the United States, and lower still in the Northern Triangle, the cost of living *relative to wages* is higher in Mexico, and higher still in the Northern Triangle.

Picture it this way: A pair of eyeglasses that costs $120 represents eight hours of labor to a waitress in the United States making $15 an hour. The same pair of glasses might cost $135 in Guatemala, and might represent *twenty-two days* of labor to a worker performing the same work, at 75 cents an hour. This is as if the pair of glasses cost $2640 to the waitress in the United States.

* Rent is also usually cheaper; local food products may be as well.

In short, what this means is that life is generally easier in the United States, harder in Mexico, and harder still in the Northern Triangle. This is the condition that the border enforces: lower prices and higher wages to the north; higher prices and lower wages to the south. Millions of people can see this clearly and act accordingly.

Now let's get into why this is the case.

One day we met three Central Americans. The Salvadoran had been traveling with his niece. He had promised his brother that he would take care of her. He was carrying her bag when Border Patrol split up their group. He was separated from her in the chaos and Border Patrol took her away. He escaped with the two Hondurans. They younger one kept telling him that he had done all he could do.

They had run out of food and water, and the older Honduran had a badly twisted knee. They had been utterly lost for four days and nights.

The Salvadoran had a cell phone that did not have service in the US. It was full of pictures of places they had been and things that they had seen. "Look at this mountain!" he said. "We crossed it! It was so beautiful. We thought for sure that we were going to die."

While they were recuperating, he asked me how much it cost to fill up the tank of our truck. I told him usually about seventy-five bucks.

"Seventy five? Dollars?"

"Yeah" I answered, assuming that he thought that this was very expensive. "How much would it cost in El Salvador?"

"A hundred and fifty, maybe two hundred."

"Two hundred? Dollars? Jesus! How much do you make an hour there?"

"I was making eight dollars a day working construction when I left."

I got a pencil and we did some math. After lengthy deliberations, we determined that:

1) $150-200 dollars a tank represents about twenty days of labor at $8 a day.
2) I usually make about $15 an hour, which is about $120 a day.
3) This meant that a $175 tank of gas for the Salvadoran was as difficult to afford as a $2500 tank of gas would be for me.

"That's a problem," I said.

"It's a very serious problem," he agreed. "They tied our currency to the dollar, and everything got incredibly expensive. It's just impossible to live there right now."

A little later he found a laminated picture of a young girl in our kitchen. "Who is this?" he asked me.

"Um, she was abandoned by her guide. One of our volunteers found her body in the desert last winter. She was only fourteen."

"Where was she from?"

"El Salvador." He looked like he was going to cry. "How old is your niece?"

"Fourteen." The younger Honduran put his arm around the Salvadoran's shoulders. "She was having a hard time keeping up. I thought I was going to have to carry her. It was dark. There were lights and screaming. Everybody was running every which way. She fell down and they grabbed her. I saw them carry her away. I ran. I don't know if she is safe. I don't know if I did the right thing."

"I'm sorry," I told him.

We ate together, and they left as the moon was coming up. The older Honduran had wrapped up his knee and taken a lot of painkillers. "No matter what happens," the Salvadoran said, "we're not going to leave him. They're not going to get us. We're going to make it." He called us a week later from his cousin's house in Utah. They had all made it out of the desert.

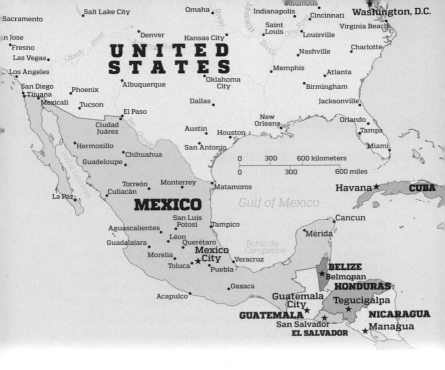

The South

What is happening south of the border that drives people north across the US border?

There's no single answer. Each case is different. Mexico, Guatemala, El Salvador, and Honduras do not comprise a homogeneous context, nor is any one of them internally homogeneous. What they have in common is that many people with citizenship in these countries cross the border to the United States to live and work, and that these workers provide American employers with much of their lowest-paid labor. South of the border, many of these same workers also provide the American economy with many of its cheap agricultural products and much of its cheap manufacturing labor. Aside from this, the four countries differ culturally, economically, historically, and in nearly every other way.

Let's look at each of them in detail.

Mexico

If you talk to some people in the United States, you get the impression that everyone who sets foot on Mexican soil is immediately robbed, decapitated, and murdered. At that rate, you'd think everyone in Mexico would be dead. In fact, one can go from one end of the country to the other, and mostly be surrounded by people calmly going about the business of their daily lives. On Christmas Eve of 2014, I was in San Cristóbal de las Casas and the air was ringing out with explosions… of firecrackers, as hundreds of cheerful people hung around the Zócalo together, playing with balloon animals and drinking *atoles* with their kids. Mexico has grave and explosive problems but it's a far cry from Syria. My suspicion is that even in Syria people are still calm and happy sometimes.

To understand the cycle of events that push and pull people across North America, we have to scrutinize the aspects of Mexico that are ugly and brutal. But that's not the only story to tell, or even the most interesting one. It would be just as edifying to write about the stunning biodiversity of Mexican punk rock, to explore the significance of the phrase *"no mames, güey,"* or to sing the praises of the seven *moles* of Oaxaca. It is true that Mexico can be dangerous, even deadly. It can also be harmonious and safe. The same can be said of Guatemala, El Salvador, Honduras, and the United States.

As I alluded to above, a slim majority of Mexican citizens that I met in the desert were crossing the border primarily to return to their homes in the United States. A considerable minority were crossing primarily to get away from the violence and instability that is sometimes referred to as the "Mexican Drug War." Virtually all were driven at least in part by the knowledge that they could make a better living in the United States. Why this particular constellation of factors?

Mexico and the United States have *history*, of course, and there's no need to reiterate it at length here. It's enough to say that Mexico has been the site of over 500 years of struggle: first against slavery and colonization, then to win independence from Spain, then to resist being absorbed by the United States, then to expel the French, then against the dictatorship of Porfirio Diaz, and recently to end the 71 years of one-party rule under the PRI (Institutional Revolutionary Party).

Mexico gained its independence as a sovereign state in 1821. By 1854, it had lost more than a third of its territory through sale and invasion by the United States, including most of what is now the American Southwest. Hence the phrase that I've heard in southern Arizona more times than I could count: "We didn't cross the border, the border crossed us."

For a long time, migrants from Mexico provided American farm owners with most of their lowest-paid agricultural labor. Many farmworkers would come to the United States seasonally, work in poor conditions for low wages, and return home. Lacking the rights of citizens, it was very difficult for them to organize to win higher wages or defend their interests as workers. This was the context in which the United Farmworkers were organizing in the 1960s. More recent efforts by migrant farmworkers to act collectively include the 1998-2004 Farm Labor Organizing Committee boycott of Mt. Olive pickles and the 2001-2005 Coalition of Immokalee Workers "A Penny More" campaign targeting Taco Bell.

The passage of the North American Free Trade Agreement (NAFTA) in 1994 changed the equation. In addition to its ruinous impact on American industrial communities, NAFTA inflicted truly catastrophic damage on Mexican agricultural communities. In preparation for the agreement, the Mexican government amended its Constitution to allow for the privatization of communally-held campesino and indigenous *ejido* land, undoing a major accomplishment of the Mexican Revolution. NAFTA then permitted heavily-subsidized American agribusiness giants such as Cargill and Archer Daniels Midland to flood the Mexican market with cheap commodities from the United States, espe-

cially corn, rendering farming untenable for millions of Mexican campesinos who could not hope to compete on such a scale.*

This was the background of the Zapatista rebellion in the southern state of Chiapas. The participants correctly identified so-called "free" trade as an existential threat to Mexican campesinos and indigenous people, predicting that this agreement would mark a final deathblow to their way of life if they failed to resist. The Zapatistas rose up in arms on New Year's Day in 1994, the same day that NAFTA went into effect. Exactly as the Zapatistas predicted, NAFTA drove millions of rural Mexicans, many of whom were already living in desperate poverty, off the land and straight into the abyss. This set off a massive wave of migration as millions of people left their homes to find work in Mexican cities, in sweatshops primarily owned by American corporations along the Mexican side of the border and across the border in the United States.

A great many Mexicans went to the United States around this time and began to set up lives there. Starting in 1994, internal deportations and border militarization on the American side increased dramatically, intensifying again after the attacks of September 11, 2001 and snowballing ever since. Border militarization has made crossing the border so difficult, expensive, traumatic, and dangerous that the former pattern of seasonal travel between Mexico and the United States is almost entirely a thing of the past. If someone makes the commitment to cross the border now, it's usually to stay for a substantial period of time. Consequently, undocumented people constitute a permanent segment of the US population, a caste without rights totaling at least several million.

* This may seem to contradict my previous statement that imported goods are often more expensive in Mexico than in the United States, but it does not. Corn is a *commodity*, which is grown in both Mexico and the United States. To dominate the Mexican market, American agribusiness must compete with Mexican growers. In this case, the point is not that American corn sells for more in Mexico than it does in the United States, but that American corn sells for less in Mexico than Mexican corn does. A version of this process in which small farmers are driven out of business and off their land has played out in the United States and many other countries around the world.

Migration from Mexico to the United States peaked at some point in the mid-2000s and has been tapering off ever since, largely due to the strength of the Mexican economy relative to that of the United States following the housing crash of 2008. Since 2012, the Pew Research Center and various other analysts have reported "net-zero" migration from Mexico to the United States. This may be statistically true, but it misses the point. Working in the desert, I met huge numbers of Mexican citizens throughout this time. This is because the American government deports untold thousands of people every year who in fact live in the United States, and most of these people will cross the border again in order to return to their homes and children. It's hard to say how many; the government is not forthcoming with these statistics. Not to put too fine a point on it, but this revolving door is not the situation that "net-zero" implies.

That's why a slim majority of Mexican citizens that I met in the desert were crossing the border to *return home.*

What is referred to as the "Mexican Drug War" is usually portrayed in the United States as an ongoing, low-intensity, asymmetric war between the Mexican government on one side and various drug-trafficking cartels on the other, with the government's principal goals being to put down drug-related violence and ultimately to dismantle the cartels. This is all wrong (except for the adjectives), and I don't believe I've ever heard a single Mexican from anywhere on the political spectrum describe the conflict to me in those terms. In fact, the conflict consists of ever-shifting alignments of state and non-state actors competing for control of the fantastically lucrative transportation industry that delivers drugs and undocumented workers to the United States. Calling it a war on drugs is like calling the invasion of Iraq a war on oil.

The war is so convoluted and the alliances between cartels and factions of the state shift so rapidly that describing them brings to mind Heisenberg's Uncertainty Principle: we can pinpoint the positions of the participants, or their properties, but never both at once.

The simplest possible version of the story is that there are two unequal centers of gravity—the more massive Sinaloa cartel and the more energetic Zetas cartel, with factions of the Mexican state as well as any number of smaller cartels affiliating with one side or the other as circumstances dictate. The war began in earnest in 2006, when the administration of then-President Felipe Calderón began to involve state forces directly in a way that they had not been involved before. It has raged on interminably ever since, and the violence in some parts of the country has been outrageous, claiming over 120,000 lives as of 2016. The places most affected have included Ciudad Juárez in Chihuahua, the central state of Jalisco, the northeastern states of Tamaulipas, Coahuila, and Nuevo León, and the southern states of Michoacán, Guerrero, Veracruz, Oaxaca, and Chiapas.

It's worth sketching out a portrait of the main actors in this drama.

The Sinaloa Cartel, based in the northwest and with agrarian roots, is a most extraordinary organization. It is probably the most successful drug-trafficking network that has ever existed, and it has demonstrated a long-term vision and a supple grasp of strategy surpassing those of many national governments. It overlaps with the government of Mexico to such an extent that it is just as correct to say that the state is part of Sinaloa as to say that Sinaloa is part of the state. Both statements are true.

Some American analysts express concern that Mexico is or may become a "failed state." They need not worry. The Mexican state has not failed—it is the most successful criminal enterprise the world has ever seen.

Sinaloa's boss of all bosses, *el jefe de jefes,* Joaquín "Chapo" Guzmán, is at 5'6" a figure of such epic proportions in the Mexican cosmos that to compare him to Robin Hood or Sauron would be to vastly overstate the stature of either of those characters. This man has (supposedly) escaped from prison twice, once in a laundry basket and once on an underground motorcycle.*As

* See *Los Señores del Narco* by Anabel Hernández for extensive evidence that the Mexican government was deeply involved in planning and executing at least the first escape.

of this writing he is (supposedly) in custody; no Mexican I have spoken to is entirely convinced.

Sinaloa portrays itself as the lesser of two evils and claims to fight a cleaner war. It accuses the Zetas of victimizing civilians and committing atrocities. "We are drug traffickers, not murderers," they say. "We don't mess with honest people." This is self-serving and in bad faith, but there is truth to it.

Sinaloa's basic strategy, elegant in its simplicity, is *plata o plomo*, silver or lead, the bribe or the bullet. Sinaloa's reputation is that it will make an offer to do things the easy way, that it will keep its promises and pay its debts, and that it will be more than capable of doing things the hard way if need be. Sinaloa is the house, and the house always wins. One cannot help mourning the fact that the people at the heart of this project—many of them the children of campesinos and undeniably organizational geniuses—did not apply their talents to radical social transformation or some other wholesome pursuit. I usually hear Sinaloa referred to in the singular.

By contrast, the Zetas cartel is based in the northeast and has its roots in the military. Members of the Mexican Army's Special Forces Corps (GAFE) founded the organization in the mid-1990s. The founders were among the roughly 500 GAFE personnel that Special Forces groups from the US, Israel, and Guatemala trained in counterinsurgency and commando operations at Ft. Bragg in North Carolina, in order to combat Zapatista rebels in Chiapas. Somewhere between 30 and 200 of these soldiers made use of this training by immediately signing on as enforcers for the Gulf Cartel, a well-established drug-trafficking organization and at that time the Sinaloa Cartel's primary rival. Before long, the Zetas became more powerful than the Gulf Cartel itself, eventually turning on their employers and striking out on their own in 2010.

The Zetas are indeed a special force. Their core cadre is composed of a rogue's gallery of mercenaries and defectors from every branch of the Mexican military and police, as well as more than a few from those of Guatemala and the United States. Armed to the teeth, rolling in cash, expertly trained and utterly without scruples, the Zetas have introduced a level of brutality into the ecosystem of Mexican organized crime surpassing anything that came before. While Sinaloa has always claimed to avoid civilian casualties, the Zetas go out of their way to incur them at every turn.

The Zetas' former captain, Heriberto "The Executioner" Lazcano, a widely known sadist generally regarded as the devil himself by anyone I've ever heard mention his name, was (supposedly) killed in Coahuila in October 2012. However, gunmen stormed the funeral home where his body was (supposedly) being held and whisked it away, never to be seen again. Nobody seems to know quite what to believe.

The Zetas cultivate an image of extreme ruthlessness, and make no pretensions to abide by any kind of ethical code. They promise to fight as dirty as possible, and they deliver. They accuse Sinaloa of rank hypocrisy, of engaging in most of the behavior that it denounces the Zetas for, and of being in collusion with the government. "We are murderers," they say, "but we are not liars." There is truth to this; in some ways, the Zetas' honesty is almost refreshing.

The Zetas' basic strategy, attractive in its way, is to overturn the board if they can't win. In a furious push to dislodge Sinaloa from its place at the top of the ladder, the Zetas have transgressed every boundary of acceptable behavior, committing such a catalog of crimes against nature, humanity, and god that it boggles the mind to recount them. In many ways prefiguring the Islamic State of Iraq and Syria (ISIS), the Zetas came to the same conclusion years earlier and half a world away: it is possible to build a fearsome army—and to make a lot of money—by putting guns in people's hands and giving them license to break every rule. It's doubtful that such nihilism could ever be part of a project of liberation, but one cannot help mourning the fact that the Zetas did not decide to unleash hell on the top of Mexican society rather than on the bottom. I usually hear the Zetas referred to in the plural.

The war can be read as an ugly perversion of a conflict that cuts to Mexico's core—the conflict between campesinos (who gave birth to Sinaloa) and the military (who gave birth to the

Zetas). The peculiar twist is that it is Sinaloa that is most closely tied to the "loyal" factions of the state, and the Zetas that are most closely tied to the "rogue" factions. Just as many Mexican soldiers are a generation removed from their agrarian roots, most of Sinaloa's leadership was born in the 1950s while most of the Zetas' leadership was born in the 1970s, a generation later. There is an air of patricide to the conflict between the two camps.*

The third term in this equation is comprised of Mexico's many social movements. A great part of the violence in Mexico is actually the repression of social movements masquerading as a drug war—especially in the south, which has long been much poorer than the capital or the north, and where those movements have traditionally been the strongest. Mexico has a rich history of radical struggle and thought. From the Caste War of Yucatán in 1847 to the Revolution and the original Zapatista movement of the 1910s, from the protests and occupations in Mexico City in 1968 to the uprisings in San Salvador Atenco and Oaxaca in 2002 and 2006, from the siege of San Juan Copala in 2010 to the self-defense forces now standing guard over Santa María Ostula and Cherán, from the modern-day Zapatistas firing the first shots in resistance to the global capitalist hegemony of the post-Cold War era more than twenty years ago to the ways that their concepts of autonomy and self-determination have informed contemporary struggles from Oakland to Rojava, Mexicans have contributed immeasurably to the project of liberation.

It is probably not a coincidence that the event that is usually viewed as the starting point of the drug war—Calderón's deployment of 6500 Mexican Army soldiers into Michoacán in December of 2006—took place within two weeks of the suppression of the uprising in Oaxaca in late November.

* In Tamaulipas and south Texas, one can advertise for the Gulf Cartel by displaying John Deere regalia. One can advertise for the Zetas by displaying Porsche regalia. The branding of the two camps is telling: part of the appeal of the Zetas is that they are "not your father's drug cartel." This same generation gap divides the leadership of Al-Qaeda (1950s) and ISIS (1970s); some of the dynamics between them are similar.

The war in Mexico is a clash of elemental forces, personified by three groups of people in black masks with guns: Order (Sinaloa), Chaos (the Zetas), and Transformation (the Zapatistas and other associated rebels). It's not clear how this war will end, or what will happen when it does, but for now it is not surprising that there are many Mexican citizens who cross the border primarily to *get away*. The world is getting smaller, though—this trialectic is playing out similarly in Syria, personified by Assad, ISIS, and the revolutionaries in Rojava.* Such conflicts are spreading, and eventually there will be nowhere left to run.

And what can be done, then? Borrowing a couple of points from the late Charles Bowden, I'll answer this as best I can from my vantage point as a solidarity worker in the United States.

The government of the United States bears a great deal of responsibility for the conflagration that has consumed Mexico over the last ten years. As I described above, by imposing NAFTA, it decimated the Mexican agricultural sector and threw millions of people who were already poor into absolute ruin. This in turn created millions of internal and external migrants and refugees, many of whom eventually turned to the cartels rather than starve. The prohibition on the use and sale of street drugs in the United States keeps the prices of these drugs artificially high, creating huge profit margins that are fought over to the south and feeding the multi-billion-dollar drug industry at the center of the conflict. By deporting hundreds of thousands of people and militarizing the border, the US government has created a human trafficking industry closely linked to the drug industry, with billions more dollars at stake. By providing the Mexican government with money, weapons, and military training, it fuels the violence from all sides—these resources invariably go rogue as both state and non-state actors use them to vie for control of

* See *A Small Key Can Open A Large Door: the Rojava Revolution,* published by Strangers in a Tangled Wilderness, for a primer on the ongoing revolution in Syrian Kurdistan, also known as Rojava. For another perspective on the Syrian uprising, read *Burning Country: Syrians in Revolution and War* by Robin Yassin-Kassab and Leila al-Shami.

these industries, not to mention for the purpose of repressing social movements.

None of this is an accident or a mistake. In fact, the war in Mexico (like the suffering in the desert) benefits identifiable sectors of society on both sides of the border.

Official policy on these matters represents the interests of those sectors, and this is not going to change any time soon. If the government of the United States really wanted to hasten the end of the war in Mexico, it could do so by ending deportations, opening the border, legalizing the use and sale of street drugs, and cutting off military aid to the Mexican state.

These actions would have other consequences, some of which I will speculate on later. However, they would take most of the oxygen out of the conflict by removing most of the profits and most of the means to fight over them.† If this took place, I have full faith that Mexicans would be able to figure out how to sort out the problems of Mexico, as they have done in the past.

Needless to say, this is not going to happen. There is no political will in Washington to take any of these actions, or from the American public outside of a radical fringe. Those of us on that fringe can try to compel the government to change its drug and immigration policies; we will probably at least succeed in shifting the grounds of the debate. It may be easier to change everything, or else to hang on while everything changes around us.

Until then, people will cross the border—whatever the risk, whatever the cost, and no matter what obstacles stand in their way. By any means necessary.

---

† Once occasionally reads commentary to the effect that lax American gun laws fuel the Mexican drug war, because cartel operatives supposedly buy guns in the United States and bring them down to Mexico. This undoubtedly does happen, but it is missing the point. The lion's share of the weapons and ammunition used by all sides in the conflict are diverted from (or used by) the various factions of the Mexican security forces: the local and federal police, the army, and so on. This hardware is not purchased at pawnshops and gun shows in Arizona and Texas and smuggled piece by piece through customs in Nogales and Matamoros; it is bought and paid for by governments, often with American tax dollars provided directly to the Mexican state.

San Salvador Atenco, in the state of México, is revered throughout Mexico for two uprisings that took place there, one in 2002 and one in 2006. In 2002, Atenco was the planned site of Mexico City's new international airport, and much of the community was slated for displacement. After ferocious clashes between police and community members organized under the umbrella of the Community Front in Defense of the Land, the government canceled the construction of the airport. It has never been built.

In May 2006, at the same time as the beginning of the uprising in Oaxaca as well as the "Day Without a Mexican" strikes and walk-outs in the United States, a second uprising erupted in Atenco following the expulsion of a group of flower vendors from the nearby Texcoco market by police. This is not as unusual as it may sound; the harassment of the millions of such *ambulantes* (precariously employed street vendors) is widespread throughout Mexico, and a source of much resentment.* The state used an overwhelming amount of violence to put down this second uprising. Over 4000 federal, state, municipal, and private police terrorized the entire community, killed two people, beat and injured many more, broke down doors and arrested 207 people without warrants, and then raped and otherwise sexually assaulted 26 women in detention. The episode remains infamous over a decade later.

A woman from San Salvador Atenco in her mid-sixties told me the following story in 2010, while we were taking part in an attempt to break the paramilitary siege of the Triqui community of San Juan Copala in Oaxaca.

"When we decided to stop the airport, we studied what the Zapatistas had done. We saw that the Zapatistas had prevailed because they had made a myth for themselves, and that they had been able to make a myth for themselves because they had a *magical outfit:* their ski masks and rifles. We knew that if we were going to stop the airport, we would need to make a

* This is basically the same course of events that led to Mohamed Bouazizi's self-immolation in Tunisia several years later, the spark that ignited the Arab Spring.

myth for ourselves as well, and that to do this we would need a *magical outfit* of our own. But we didn't know what this would be. It couldn't be that of the Zapatistas—that would make no sense. We're not Mayans, we're not guerrillas, we don't live in the jungle. We're campesinos from a small town outside of Mexico City. What could our magical outfit be? We argued about it for days, weeks even. And finally we found it: a cowboy hat, a red bandana, and a machete. Once we found our magical outfit we were unstoppable, and the airport was doomed."

To this day, residents of San Salvador Atenco can be seen with cowboy hats, red bandanas, and machetes on the barricades of struggles across Mexico. When they show up, it feels like the cavalry has arrived.

SERVICIO

F.P.D.T.
FELIPE VIVE
ATENCO VIVE
ATENCO REBELDE
NO SE RINDE NI SE VENDE

Guatemala

As I said, I've met more Mexican citizens crossing the border to return to their old life in the United States than to start a new life there. With Guatemalan citizens it's the other way around. Why?

Guatemala has been governed by a feudal system ever since colonization. To this day, the country is dominated by a small group of light-skinned families (known as the "seven families," the "oligarchy," or the "deep state") who have managed power since their European descendants arrived in the Americas. They have lorded it over the indigenous majority for more than 500 years. These families control the military and the vast majority of land and wealth, dividing major monopolies between them. The old elite is linked to coffee, sugar, and banana exports, cattle ranching, mining, and some heavy industry, such as cement production. A newer elite is linked to drug smuggling and human trafficking. Guatemalan political parties align with these competing interests.*

One hundred years ago, there was a revolution in Mexico. It ended the feudal system and laid the groundwork for the foundation of a modern state, for better or for worse. This never happened in Guatemala. The country is not governed by people who have the well-being of Guatemalan citizens at heart. In contrast to their counterparts in Mexico, the oligarchs do not uphold their end of a social contract, and they make no real pretensions to do so.

Yet, like Mexico, Guatemala is not a failed state. The government has a job to do, and it has done it well for centuries. It supplies the United States with sugar, bananas, and coffee, and

* *Partido Patriota* was in office for much of the 2010s and is now in disgrace. It was aligned with the military and various factions of the deep state, it favored orange, and its symbol was a clenched fist. As of 2016, these same people are back again, although they now prefer blue and their new party is called *Frente de Convergencia Nacional.* Like a scary clown, the Guatemalan oligarchs have a mask for every occasion. It's no secret who is the real power behind the throne. On the other hand, I've heard any number of Guatemalans bluntly describe *LIDER* (*Libertad Democrática Renovada*, Renewed Democratic Liberty) as "the narco party." It's always in the running, and favors red.

it prevents indigenous people from placing the seven families on boats and sending them back to Spain. The government has carried out this duty in the only way possible: with machine guns, helicopters, and flamethrowers.

So, instead of a revolution, Guatemala endured an almost unfathomably brutal 36-year civil war. The CIA set the wheels in motion in 1954 when they sponsored a coup that overthrew then-President Jacobo Árbenz in retribution for his attempts to redistribute land. The immensely powerful American-owned United Fruit Company[†] opposed land reform, and the CIA acted on their behalf. Denied any other route to social change, an assortment of indigenous, campesino, student, union, and leftist groups commenced armed struggle against the state in 1960. The conflict was fueled for decades by the financial and military support that the American government provided to a succession of Guatemalan military regimes. These regimes perpetrated a catalog of massacres, disappearances, torture, and other acts of state terror against the civil society of Guatemala, culminating in the "scorched earth" policy of genocide against the Mayan indigenous population during the rule of Efraín Ríos Montt in the early 1980s. Approximately 200,000 civilians lost their lives during the war; indigenous people suffered disproportionately. Armed conflict ended in December 1996 with the signing of the peace accords between the umbrella organization of guerrilla groups (Guatemalan National Revolutionary Unity or URNG) and the Guatemalan state.

Hundreds of thousands of Guatemalans fled to Mexico and the United States during the 1980s. Most had to do so illegally, since the Reagan administration—which was arming and funding the primary perpetrators of the violence—refused to recognize those exiled as refugees under American law.[‡] Many of these refugees and their families established lives in the United States and have been there ever since.

† Today, this company is known as Chiquita.

‡ Participants in the American "Sanctuary" movement assisted thousands of Guatemalans on their journey north during this time. Twenty years later some of the same people went on to form No More Deaths.

Twenty years later, peace may be worse than war. I've actually heard Guatemalans say this. As of 2016, Guatemala has the highest rate of chronic malnutrition in the Western Hemisphere, the fourth highest in the entire *world*. Chronic malnutrition affects 47% of all children, 55% of all people in rural areas, 69% of indigenous people, and 70% of indigenous children. In some villages, that number rises to 90%.* Food insecurity has been found to be the single biggest factor driving migration from the country, according to a recent report published by the International Organisation of Migration and the United Nations World Food Programme. Based on what I have seen firsthand and heard from Guatemalans, I concur.

We are talking about a country with extensive economic, political, cultural, and military ties to the United States; which is blessed with fertile soil, plentiful water, a favorable climate, and abundant natural resources; whose markets are overflowing with fruits and vegetables, and which exports well over a billion dollars of food to the north every year. Peace in Guatemala is the peace of a graveyard, plundered by thieves and haunted by the ghosts of hungry children.

About sixty percent of Guatemalans identify as indigenous. Twenty-six different languages are spoken in the country, there are many places where Spanish is not the dominant language, and there is a great deal of cultural diversity between the different indigenous groups. Indigenous people make up a more prominent part of Guatemalan society than almost anywhere else in North America. In Mexico, for instance, a substantial part of the population is indigenous as well, but nowhere near as much as in Guatemala, except in some parts of Oaxaca and Chiapas.

* This is significantly higher than in Honduras and Nicaragua, both of which are significantly poorer than Guatemala. Haiti is the poorest country in the Western Hemisphere and the average Guatemalan earns four times more than the average Haitian, but Guatemala's childhood malnutrition rates are twice as high as Haiti's. The inequality in Guatemala is positively diabolical. The source of these statistics is the report cited below.

> "When I go around America and I see the bulk of the white people, they do not feel oppressed. They feel powerless. When I go amongst my own people, we do not feel powerless. We feel oppressed. We do not want to make the trade. We see the physical genocide they are attempting to inflict upon our lives and we understand the psychological genocide they have already inflicted upon their own people."
> – John Trudell, Paha Sapa, July 18, 1980

Racism is extremely pronounced in every aspect of Guatemalan society. The derogatory terms used by *criollos* (those of mostly European ancestry) and *ladinos* (those of mixed European and indigenous ancestry) to refer to *indigenas* (those of mostly indigenous ancestry, and particularly those who do not speak Spanish as a first language) carry as much historical weight as do the terms that are used by white people to refer to Black people in the United States. This is true in Mexico as well, but it is even more pronounced in Guatemala. Most of the worst atrocities of the war were ordered by *criollos* (who commanded the army), carried out by *ladinos* (who made up the bulk of the army), and inflicted on *indigenas* (who made up the bulk of the *guerrilla* as well as the civilian population).

The peace accords of 1996 mark a complicated watershed in Guatemalan history. For nearly forty years, the guerrillas, most of whom were indigenous Mayans, stood up to a truly ruthless and unprincipled foe backed by the full weight of the American government. The guerrillas did not exactly win, but neither did they entirely lose, and when they finally did lay down their arms it was not without extracting some meaningful concessions from the Guatemalan state. One of the more important of these concessions was Convention 169 of the peace accords, which writes communal land stewardship into Guatemalan law. Legally speaking, a lot of Guatemalan land is not owned privately by individuals or corporations, nor publicly by the state, but communally by the indigenous people who occupy it.

Furthermore, under Convention 169, resource extraction issues on communal land have to be decided by communal processes. This means that if a mining company wants to mine for gold on communal land, it cannot simply buy the land; nor can the state just lease it out. A popular assembly of the community involved has to approve the project, and this permission often turns out to be difficult to obtain. This aspect of Guatemalan environmental and indigenous law can provide stronger protection against extractive industries than either Mexican or American law usually does. Imagine if the United States Forest Service had to go through a community assembly every time it wanted to lease out public land to a logging company! It took 36 years of armed struggle to win this concession.

Unsurprisingly, however, these parts of the peace accord have been consistently abrogated by a long succession of venal and corrupt post-war governments, who have tried their best to auction off the country to the highest bidder.

Nonetheless, indigenous people have *power* in Guatemala, in a way that is very different from what one sees in the United States or even most of Mexico. On the day of the World Cup final in 2014, the Guatemalan Congress tried to slip through a piece of legislation called the Monsanto Law, which would have given exclusivity on patented seeds to a handful of transnational companies. Indigenous groups blockaded Congress, refusing to let in food or water or to let anyone out to sleep or use the bath-room until the law was repealed, which it was. It is very difficult to imagine this happening in Washington, DC or Mexico City.

Resource extraction is a major issue in Guatemala. In the western highland provinces of San Marcos and Huehuetenango in particular, along the border with the Mexican state of Chiapas, there is a great deal of active mining (primarily gold, silver, and copper), as well as many more locations where transnational corporations are attempting to push licenses for new mining projects through the popular assemblies.*

Guatemala has an extensive history of resistance to resource exploitation, especially in these regions. Both state and private police, as well as military and para-military forces, have jailed and murdered many opponents of mining and other megaprojects there.

Not coincidentally, many of the Guatemalans I have met crossing the border turn out to be coming from these parts of the country—San Marcos and Huehuetenango. I've seen evidence firsthand to suggest that mining companies, the drug cartels, and the Guatemalan state have been colluding to cleanse parts of these areas of inhabitants in order to clear the way for megaprojects, drug smuggling, and human trafficking. I'll return to this later.

The vast majority of the cocaine from South America also passes through the Mexican-Guatemalan border on the way to the United States, along with all undocumented Central American migrants and refugees. As in Mexico, both state and non-state actors compete for control of the drug smuggling and human trafficking industries built up around the border. This plays out no less violently in Guatemala. Add on top of that the truly frightening levels of murder and violent crime in some parts of the country (much of it an extension of El Salvador's

* Many of the companies involved with mining in Guatemala are Canadian-owned. One of the best-known examples is the Marlin gold mine in San Marcos near the indigenous Mam municipalities of Sipacapa and San Miguel Ixtahuacán, which is owned by a Guatemalan subsidiary of the Canadian company Goldcorp. See the 2005 documentary *Sipakapa No Se Vende (Sipakapa Is Not For Sale),* directed by Alvaro Revenga.

gang problems—see below) and, long story short, the place is a mess. I've met numerous Guatemalans who have told me that the oligarchy has fomented general social violence in order to justify the use of a "strong hand" to quell the chaos: the hand of the Guatemalan military, which was deeply discredited after the war.

On top of all of this, at least speaking from my personal experience, Guatemala is profoundly dysfunctional, in a way that Mexico is not. Teachers don't get paid, nurses don't get paid, hospitals don't have sufficient medicine or equipment, the justice system is a shambles, the government is corrupt on every level and everybody knows it, there's virtually no legal work in much of the country, there are loose dogs cannibalizing each other in trash heaps, and in general the state does even less for people than it does in Mexico. The government won't put out fires if they are burning in places where indigenous people live.*

None of the issues that led to the internal armed conflict in Guatemala have been resolved. All of the components of a future war are there, waiting to explode. An entire generation of armed struggle is no walk in the park, and the fatigue is still palpable twenty years later. This is one noticeable difference between Guatemalan and Mexican society. I've often heard Mexicans, even those who do not ascribe to radical politics, say things like "The situation in my country is untenable; maybe we need another revolution." I've often heard Guatemalans, even those who do ascribe to radical politics, say things like "I just hope we can address the problems in my country without having to go to war again." I fear for what the future holds for my friends there.

* My friends and I spent almost two weeks of January 2015 putting out a forest fire that was burning above their village and threatening the town water supply. We did this with machetes and shovels, with no protective equipment whatsoever, and with burning boulders rolling down the mountain above us. The Guatemalan government refused to send a helicopter from the capital to douse the flames. The forest had not burned in living memory, I was told. Everyone said that it was a consequence of climate change. Droughts connected to climate change are contributing to deforestation, disrupting crop cycles, and exacerbating food insecurity in Guatemala.

That being said, the biggest thing to happen in Guatemala in recent years was probably the widespread protests that brought down the government of the most recent ex-president, Otto Pérez Molina, in September 2015. Pérez Molina was a former army general who personally coordinated massacres in the indigenous area of the "Ixíl Triangle" during the Ríos Montt years. He was elected in 2011 on a remarkably unsubtle platform: "a strong hand" was both his campaign slogan and the symbol of his political party (*Partido Patriota*). As it turns out, he and most of his administration spent much of their time in office overseeing a corruption scheme that came to be known as "La Linea," in which the Guatemalan customs agency offered importers greatly reduced tariffs in exchange for kickbacks that were shared among dozens of government officials. When this story went public, massive protests broke out across the country, eventually gaining so much momentum that Pérez Molina, his son-in-law, the then-vice-president Roxana Baldetti, and dozens of other high-ranking officials all ended up not only unemployed but in jail.

Although it is more than a little perverse that Pérez Molina was finally brought to account for graft rather than for personally coordinating acts of genocide, it was still unprecedented in Guatemala, where it is unheard of for a sitting president and ex-general to be brought down by street protests—much less without massive bloodshed. While this was heartening, most Guatemalans I know believe that part of what happened was that the military and the oligarchy came to see Pérez Molina as an embarrassment, abandoned him, and began to prepare the figure of his successor, Jimmy Morales, the current president and literally an ex-clown. It's not clear what is going to happen next.

In short, this is why so many people are leaving their old lives in Guatemala: to get away from widespread conditions of poverty and instability.

The Guatemalan guerrilla movement had a largely unrecognized influence on world affairs by directly inspiring the aesthetic of the

Zapatista rebellion and by profoundly informing and prefiguring the rebellion itself. Chiapas directly borders Guatemala; it is also heavily Mayan. From the ski masks and pseudonyms to the illuminating realization that the seizure of state power is not actually a revolutionary project, many aspects of the Zapatista movement can be seen as extensions of, reactions to, or lessons learned from the Guatemalan civil war. The Zapatistas deserve tremendous credit for applying these lessons correctly, but it's worth remembering that the image that they made irresistible was that of something that the Guatemalan guerrillas actually did for nearly forty years.

The *guerrilla* and all of the suffering and sacrifices that its participants endured have been largely forgotten outside of Guatemala, but through the Zapatistas its influence can still be seen across the world today.

El Salvador

El Salvador is smaller than Guatemala, more densely populated, and less indigenous. In marked contrast to Guatemala or even Mexico, the population is nearly entirely *ladino*. In El Salvador, once again, there was a brutal civil war from 1979 to 1990 that claimed around 80,000 lives. Once again, the American government backed a succession of military regimes that committed a series of massacres, disappearances, rapes, bombings, torture, collective reprisals, and other atrocities on the public at large. The most infamous single incident was probably the murder of over 800 civilians in the village of El Mozote by the Salvadoran army on December 11, 1981.

In El Salvador, even more so than in Guatemala, it is probable that the coalition of guerrilla groups (the Faribundo Martí National Liberation Front or FMLN) would have succeeded in overthrowing the Salvadoran government were it not for the intervention of the American state. As much as a quarter of the entire country fled the war during the 1980s, mostly to the United States, again often with assistance from the Sanctuary movement. The war formally ended with the signing of the peace agreement in 1992; about two million Salvadorans now live in the United States—roughly a fifth of the entire population.

In my observation, El Salvador is noticeably more well off than either Guatemala or Honduras, if less so than Mexico. Three to five billion dollars in remittances pour into the very small country yearly from Salvadoran workers in the United States—perhaps a fifth of the total GDP. One can find separate bins for trash, compost, and recycling in many municipal parks, there are fewer stray dogs, and generally speaking it looks like a grittier version of the United States rather than a different world entirely. Also, in 2009, the FMLN was elected to power for the first time since the end of the war, and for a while behaved themselves somewhat better than the right-wing governments in Guatemala and Honduras. So it could be tempting to view El Salvador as a regional success story.

However, this is where the story gets complicated. Various Salvadoran street gangs formed in refugee communities in Los Angeles during and after the war, at first based at least in part on a legitimate need to carve out some place for Salvadorans in the not-very-welcoming atmosphere of riot-era LA. The most prominent of these gangs became Mara Salvatrucha (MS-13) and Barrio 18 (M18). Thousands of members of both groups were eventually deported back to El Salvador, where they began to fight each other for territory.

It is incorrect to understand MS-13 and M18 as monolithic organizations. Rather, they are franchised and dispersed networks consisting of numerous cliques and factions. That being said, the gangs exert tremendous influence over daily life in much of El Salvador; in many places, they possess power comparable to that of the state. Gang members are the sole or primary breadwinners in many poor and working-class Salvadoran households, and in many neighborhoods the gangs function as the sole employer and de facto police. There are numerous downsides to this system, the most serious being that the three-sided conflict between MS-13, M18, and the government has made El Salvador one of the most violent places on the planet outside of an active warzone.

> "To focus on stopping the migration without stopping the pain that drives it (and especially when your own country has helped foster much of that pain) is like an arsonist setting fire to a building and then blocking the exits as folks try and escape."
> – *Tim Wise*

In March 2012, a truce was negotiated between the three parties, negotiated by former FMLN rebel and congressman Raul Mijango, the Minister of Public Security and Justice David Munguía Payés, and Monsignor Fabio Colindres, a bishop of the Catholic Church. Although it is not clear exactly how this transpired, it appears that the government agreed to a variety of concessions, including the repeal of the Gang Prohibition Act, the return of the army to the barracks, the end of police operations in territory controlled by the gangs, the repeal of a law which provided benefits in exchange for information about people with criminal ties, and a series of improvements in prisoners' quality of life. In exchange for this, it appears that the mostly-imprisoned leadership of MS-13 and M18 agreed to a cessation of hostilities between themselves and with the state.

Practically overnight, homicides dropped from fourteen a day to five. The truce held at least in part for nearly three years, and by most accounts I've heard the country was pretty livable for a while. We saw the results on the border immediately, where we met far fewer Salvadorans crossing the desert during that time.

However, the truce had completely broken down by 2015, for complicated reasons involving intransigence and duplicity on all sides—including that of the US government, which was never remotely excited about the arrangement, presumably being of the opinion that a stable and prosperous El Salvador governed by the FMLN and aligned with Venezuela and the South American "Pink Tide" was not actually a desirable outcome. Violence spiraled out of control in 2015, reaching levels not seen since the worst of the civil war or almost anywhere else in the world outside of Syria, Iraq, and the Central African Republic.

Under serious domestic pressure to restore some semblance of order, the FMLN resorted to tactics borrowed from its enemies during the war: night raids, mass imprisonment, and collective punishment. When this happened, the gangs did not take it lying down, responding with a vigorous and concerted campaign of assassinations of police and soldiers, as well as car bombings targeting police stations and other government installations—a tactic rarely if ever seen even in the most unstable parts of Mexico.

The Salvadoran government and press, in turn, have begun to use a language of "terrorism" and existential "warfare" against "enemy combatants" when speaking about the conflict. This is ironic, considering that the government is in no small part comprised of people who were once labeled terrorists and criminals—as many gang members and some of the more reflective parts of the FMLN itself have repeatedly pointed out. A web search combining *mareros* or *pandilleros* with *cucarachas* turns up endless and blood-curdling commentary from presumably middle-and-upper-class Salvadorans describing gang members as cockroaches and intimating that the only solution is to "kill them all." This is all the more frightening because it has happened before in El Salvador. Various Salvadorans have told me that it is not impossible that some of the bombings may be false-flag actions designed by such elements to justify "social cleansing." One shudders to think what may happen when the right gets back into power.

Unsurprisingly, in 2015 we saw a surge in the numbers of Salvadorans crossing the desert, nearly all reporting similar conditions back home and expressing some version of a similar desire to get away from the mayhem consuming their country.

At the risk of being repetitive, it's worth driving home how much responsibility the government of the United States bears in creating this mess. First, it bankrolled the Salvadoran right wing in its war on the better half of its own society. Then, it deported thousands of the survivors of this war dead broke back to a country the size of Massachusetts that it had just destroyed. Most recently, it undermined the efforts of the FMLN and the gangs to come to a workable compromise. After all this, it was very unlikely that anything could have happened except for El Salvador to go up in flames.

The following story is well known in El Salvador if not in much of the rest of the world.

The man who ordered the massacre at El Mozote was an especially revolting character by the name of Lieutenant Colonel Domingo Monterrosa Barrios, commander at the time of the Atlacatl Battalion, an elite counter-insurgency unit of the Salvadoran Army. This battalion, which carried out the massacre, was created in 1980 at the United States Army School of the Americas in Panama, and trained in Fort Bragg, North Carolina by US Special Forces. Monterrosa graduated from the School of the Americas, like most of his ilk across the region.*

According to Mark Danner's account of the incident in *The Massacre at El Mozote,* Monterrosa was known to be unusually obsessed with destroying Radio Venceremos, the FMLN radio station that specialized in news of the war, acerbic commentary, and pointed ridicule of the government. Radio Venceremos had mocked and denounced him personally on endless occasions; the radio station had become a potent symbol, operating for years inside territory that Monterossa claimed to control.

Monterrosa's career was ended in October 1984, by an elaborate ruse. A small FMLN unit carried a radio transmitter to an area patrolled by army troops, was then "discovered" by the soldiers,

* See SOA Watch at soaw.org for more information on the School of the Americas.

exchanged fire, "suffered casualties,"[†] and was then "forced" to "evacuate" the position and "abandon" the transmitter. Radio Venceremos went off the air immediately, and the following day Monterrosa convened national and international press in the city of San Miguel, announcing triumphantly that the radio station was no more. Monterrosa went to the northeastern town of Joateca, loaded the trophy into his personal helicopter by hand, and took off for the press conference, accompanied by five other commanders of the Atlacatl Battalion, including his direct successor. Apparently, the chief American military advisor on the scene turned down the ride.

The transmitter contained eight sticks of dynamite and a detonator activated by air pressure. The helicopter and everyone inside of it was blown out of the sky as it passed over guerrilla positions near El Mozote, where presumably the molecules of Monterrosa's body mingled with those of the 800 people whose deaths he had ordered.

The remnants of the helicopter are still on display at the Museum of the Revolution in the municipality of Perquín, not far from where the massacre took place. I can attest that haggard ex-combatants there still tell this tale with great relish.

Honduras

I have spent much less time in Honduras than Mexico, Guate- mala, or El Salvador.

At the risk of lapsing into extreme informality, I will say this: when standing on the Salvadoran or Nicaraguan side of the border holding a piece of refuse, one can normally say, "Hmm, where should I put this empty water bottle? Ah, perhaps in that trash can!" On the Honduran side, it's more like "Well, I guess I'll just throw it on the ground, which is what absolutely

† In fact, blood from a rooster was left on the scene. As far as I know, this brave creature was the only collateral damage of the operation.

everybody else is doing since there's no other option. And look at that army guy with a huge assault rifle! And that other one! And those other ones!"

Of course, I would prefer to see the garbage collected by de-centralized networks of friends than by the state, but it does seem to be the worst of both worlds when the state clearly exists, has the capacity to place huge numbers of American-made M-16s in the hands of god-knows-who, but also demonstrates no interest whatsoever in providing the most basic health, sanitation, education, social welfare, or waste management services to the population.

That, in a nutshell, is modern Honduras. Combining the poverty of Nicaragua, the dysfunction of Guatemala, and the violence of El Salvador, but lacking the recent legacy of at-least-partially-successful efforts to address the country's problems through armed struggle that characterizes all three of those places, Honduras is currently a case study in everything bad in this part of the world.

There was a 1950s-style coup in Honduras in 2009 backed by the government of the United States, and things appear to have been unremittingly messed up ever since. We have met an enormous number of Hondurans crossing the border in the years since the coup, out of all proportion to the size of the country. In 2012, for instance, less than half of the people that I met on the border came from Mexico, Guatemala, or El Salvador, and more than half came from Honduras—despite the fact that Mexico alone has a population sixteen times the size of Honduras. We heard different versions of the same story from countless people: grinding poverty, chronic hunger and malnutrition, widespread violence and insecurity (much of it an extension of El Salvador's gang problems), a rampant HIV/AIDS epidemic, appalling levels of violence against women and LGBTQ people, assassinations of environmentalists, union organizers, and human rights advocates,[*] and a lack of the most basic services or opportunities.

Let me emphasize this one more time. If Honduras is in shambles, it is not because Hondurans are any less resourceful

* For example, the recent assassination of Berta Cáceres.

or fundamentally decent than anyone else, or even because its rulers are any more wretched and callous than our own. It is because the structure of the North American economy has made any other outcome impossible.

One of my most cherished belongings is a Honduran basketball jersey given to me with pride by a teenager I met in the desert, who eventually made it home to her loving and supportive family in Los Angeles. I hope to see the day when my Honduran friends have the option of a decent life in their place of birth, whether it takes a revolution in Honduras, the United States, or both.

Tensions

Many people in the United States are unaware of how much tension exists between the societies of Mexico and Central America, or of the degree to which Mexicans and Central Americans do not on the whole think of themselves as the same people.

Perhaps it will be easiest to illustrate this using soccer. During the World Cup, practically any Central American soccer fan will root for any Central American team against any other team in the world. So in 2014, Guatemalans overwhelmingly rooted for Honduras versus France, and millions of Nicaraguans celebrated Costa Rica's string of victories despite the significant tension between the two societies. However, practically any Central American soccer fan will root *against* the Mexican team, and for *any* team opposing it. So Guatemalans everywhere cheered when the Netherlands knocked Mexico out of the Cup. This tendency seems to trump even memories of war; in my observation, Salvadoran and Guatemalan soccer fans will overwhelmingly and unreservedly root for the United States over Mexico in a head-to-head match. I have watched less soccer in Mexico, but it seems to me that, similarly, most Mexicans will root for *anyone* over the United States, up to and including Spain.

Central Americans, especially migrants and refugees, are on the whole treated horrendously in Mexico, subject to systematic mistreatment by every government body and unfortunately by some of the public as well.* If pressed, many Central Americans, even those who ascribe to radical politics, will express a blanket suspicion of Mexicans in general. That being said, there are countless organizations and individuals in Mexico working in meaningful and concrete solidarity with Central Americans. In my observation, the dynamics are acknowledged and well understood by a great many Mexicans.

As is often the case, these barriers can break down under crisis. While working in the desert, I've seen mixed groups of Mexicans and Central Americans save each others' lives, sustain each other through unimaginable hardship, and generally enjoy each other's company. However, I've also seen many examples to the contrary, and the tensions are real.

There is also a byzantine web of ugly stereotypes internal to both Mexico and Central America. To hear it in Mexico, the *norteños* are rich, stuck-up, trigger-happy gangster-cowboys; the *chilangos* in the capital use entirely too much foul language (this may actually be true); and the *sureños* are short, brown, and poor. In Guatemala, *altiplenses* know *costeños* to be hustlers, and while Salvadorans are respected it is always considered possible that they may be murderers. Salvadorans often look down on Hondurans, although unfortunately they are not alone in this. Over-the-top Mexican displays of nationalism, similar in many ways to what one sees in the United States, come off as grating and bizarre to Central Americans, half of whom took up arms against their own governments within recent memory.

This does not even begin to touch on subcultural dynamics; Americans who think of all Mexicans as straight-laced construction workers may be surprised to find that Mexico City is the freakiest place on the planet. People south of the border are not all the same.

---

* This is common enough knowledge that there is a song called *Tres Veces Mojado* about it by Los Tigres del Norte, who can be understood as Mexico's equivalent of Bruce Springsteen and The Beatles rolled into one.

The Trip

Based on my own experiences and my discussions with countless travelers, permit me to hazard a rough overview of the journey from south to north.

The trip to the border plays out very differently depending on how much money a person has and whether the person is Mexican or Central American. Let's start with Central Americans.

Citizens of Guatemala, El Salvador, Honduras, and Nicaragua can circulate freely inside of these four countries (the "CA-4"), so Salvadorans and Hondurans can travel through Guatemala to the Mexican border without any particular issues other than paying for transportation. The Mexican border, however, is another matter entirely. Citizens of the CA-4 cannot just walk up to the Mexican border and cross it without issue, nor can they circulate inside of Mexico without risk of deportation if they do not have the relevant visa. There are legal means for Central Americans to enter and pass through Mexico on the way to the United States, all which come at a price—essentially a series of bribes—that some can pay and others cannot. I will start by describing what people do when they cannot enter Mexico legally.

Mexico's heavily forested southern border is well policed, but it is relatively porous—and the authorities policing it are fantastically corrupt. Central Americans have several options for crossing it and then crossing Mexico itself. The worst and most deservedly notorious way to get to the United States is via *La Bestia* (The Beast), the Mexican freight trains. I have heard an astonishing array of horror stories about this trip; it's fair to say that for many people, crossing Mexico is an even more harrowing ordeal than crossing the border into the United States.

There are two main train lines running from southern Mexico into *La Lecheria*, the main transfer point in Mexico City for all traffic coming from the south and going north. One of these lines starts in the city of Tenosique in Tabasco, the other in Arriaga in Chiapas. So Central Americans who cannot afford any other option have to cross the Mexican border on foot and walk to one of these cities—no small distance. Every step of the way, they run the risk of robbery, rape, kidnapping, assault, extortion, deportation, arrest, and murder at the hands of the police, the military, any number of different gangs and cartels, and god knows who else; they also risk exhaustion and exposure. Common departure points in Guatemala include parts of the provinces of San Marcos and Huehuetenango (en route to Arriaga), and parts of the *Parque Nacional Sierra del Lacandón* and *Parque Nacional Laguna del Tigre* in the northern Petén (en route to Tenosique). There are shelters and solidarity projects in both cities, the most prominent being "*La 72*" in Tenosique.* From either location, it is finally possible to get on a northbound train.

Running the gauntlet across Mexico on La Bestia may be the most deadly method of travel in the entire Western Hemisphere. All of the above risks are magnified on the trains, along with the danger of death and dismemberment from falling off the freight cars, which are often incredibly overcrowded.

There are other shelters and solidarity projects along both rail lines, as well as in Mexico City and around La Lecheria itself. These projects range from established campaigns to the daily efforts of individuals and families that live along the tracks and toss food and water onto the trains as they roll by.

Once again, there are two main ways to go north from La Lecheria, both fraught with all the perils described above—including an ever-increasing risk of arrest and deportation as one proceeds further north. The first route, toward the Lower Rio Grande Valley in Texas, proceeds up to San Luis Potosí and then to Nuevo Laredo or Reynosa in Tamaulipas. The second, toward the southern Arizona desert, is through Guadalajara and then up the Pacific coast to Altar or Caborca in Sonora.

These are probably the two most important destination points for migrants and refugees along the entire border: Reynosa and Altar. Both routes have advantages and disadvantages; the problem is that ultimately both options are terrible.

The advantages of the northeastern route to Reynosa are

* See la72.org for information on how to volunteer.

that it is a much shorter trip on the train and that the terrain is somewhat less deadly on the American side. It is also closer to the eastern and mid-western parts of the United States. The disadvantage is that most of this territory is controlled by the Zetas cartel. This route is notorious for the first San Fernando Massacre of August 2010, in which the Zetas murdered 72 Central American migrants and refugees in the municipality of San Fernando just south of Matamoros in Tamaulipas,[†] and then the *second* San Fernando Massacre of April 2011, in which the Zetas hijacked numerous passenger buses on Mexican Federal Highway 101 in the same small town, kidnapping, torturing, and murdering 193 people. In southern Arizona, we saw a surge in the numbers of Central Americans crossing the desert that lasted for about two years after the San Fernando massacres, as thousands of people understandably decided that the northeastern route wasn't worth the risk.

The advantage of the northwestern route to Altar is that this territory is controlled lock, stock, and barrel by the Sinaloa cartel, who have a reputation for being more *businesslike,* if nothing else. It is also closer to the western parts of the United States. The disadvantages are that it is a much longer trip on the train, and it means crossing the border into the Sonoran Desert in southern Arizona—which has been swallowing people alive by the thousands.

Backing up, there are also many Central Americans who don't have to take the train. Central Americans who can afford to do so can pay through the cartel system to arrange for any combination of a guide through the Mexican border, passage through Mexico to the American border (most commonly to Reynosa or Altar, although there are other destinations, notably Sonoyta and Mexicali), and a guide through the American border to the other side. The disadvantage to this approach is that it can cost upwards of $10,000 with no guarantee of success. Not everyone has this money, and it represents a major expenditure to nearly all who do. It also means putting one's life completely

† *La 72,* the migrant shelter in Tenosique, is named in their honor.

in the hands of the cartel system, which entails real dangers of kidnapping, extortion, rape, and so on. Nevertheless, such arrangements are very common.

Then there is the possibility of risking the buses in Mexico. I have met people who did this successfully, or were able to bribe their way out of trouble when discovered. The problem is that the Mexican immigration authorities inspect northbound buses at points throughout Mexico, especially near the Guatemalan and American borders. Even I can usually tell Mexicans and Central Americans apart by overhearing a snippet of conversation, and the Mexican authorities are famously adept at this. Without even checking for papers, they can usually trip up most people with a couple of questions and demands, such as "How much do you weigh?" (Guatemalans think in pounds, Mexicans in kilograms) or "Recite for me the *Grito de Dolores*!" (virtually all Mexicans can do so, just as virtually anyone who grew up in the United States could rattle off the Pledge of Allegiance if forced to, whereas most people who grew up elsewhere could not), or through any number of other tricks. People who look indigenous invariably attract more attention. If discovered on buses, the risk of abuse at the hands of the authorities is tremendous.

Next, sometimes Central Americans can get the papers needed to cross Mexico legally. This involves jumping through numerous bureaucratic hoops, all of which are designed to separate travelers from as much money as possible, and all of which are applied in a way that systematically disfavors indigenous people. That said, there are occasions when the Mexican authorities seem to throw up their hands and essentially say "To hell with it, here are your papers, get through here as quickly as possible and you're the Americans' problem." This was happening especially frequently for a period from late 2013 to early 2014, around the time that the American press started reporting on the Central American "unaccompanied minors crisis," described below.

It's not impossible for Central Americans to get papers to enter the United States legally, but the process is exceptionally onerous. For context, any American can enter Guatemala free of charge, without a visa. US citizens can stay in the CA-4 for 90 days, and must then leave for two days by crossing the border into Chiapas, Belize, or Costa Rica before returning for another 90 days. This can be repeated forever. There are American expats around Lake Atitlán who have been doing it for decades. While it is theoretically possible for an American to be turned back by Guatemalan immigration, I have only ever heard of this happening to people who got involved in Guatemalan politics, or to people who failed to obey the "90/2" rule. Otherwise, even axe murderers are welcome.

For a Guatemalan to *apply* for a visa to visit the United States, the fee is $160, paid to the American government. This fee is not returned if the visa is denied, but the Guatemalan is welcome to try (and to pay) again. Applying for the visa means first getting a passport, which costs $160, paid to the Guatemalan government. Without fail, this must be accompanied by a bribe, paid to someone at the passport office. The bribe has to be larger if the Guatemalan is indigenous—probably about $160 more. The visa application must be filled out online, and in English. It is also timed. It probably goes without saying that most Guatemalans do not simultaneously have $500 to burn, speedy internet access, and the ability to fill out a form in English. There is a cottage industry of people who fill out these forms for a hefty fee.

Despite all this, every business day at the American embassy in Guatemala City, up to a thousand people wait in line for a hearing with a consular official. The hearing lasts three to five minutes. The most important thing is to demonstrate "binding economic ties" to Guatemala—chiefly, property ownership. If the visa is granted, it does *not* give the Guatemalan permission to enter the United States. It gives permission to present oneself legally at an American port of entry. The final decision is then made by the Customs and Border Protection agent working the port. This agent can deny the Guatemalan entry without cause, and there is no legal redress if they choose to do so. The process is equally onerous for other Central Americans, somewhat less so for Mexicans. Only a very dense person would miss the point that this system is rigged to filter out poor people.

To wrap this up, Mexicans can travel freely in Mexico without any particular issue other than paying for transportation. That said, many of the poorest Mexicans also ride the trains, on which they are subject to all the same dangers and hardships as Central Americans, aside from the threat of deportation.

Most other Mexicans traveling to the United States ride buses to Altar, Reynosa, or one of the other well-known departure points along the border.

Toward the end of 2013, we started getting calls from bus stations in Arizona, asking us to help them assist Central American women and minors who had been dropped off *by Border Patrol*. These women and children all had basically the same story to tell: they had been apprehended in the desert, detained, processed, given notices to appear in immigration court some months ahead, driven to the bus station, and told to be on their way. This was the "unaccompanied minors crisis."

This is not normal behavior on the part of Border Patrol by a long shot. For years, we had strongly condemned Border Patrol for their practice of depositing Central Americans directly across the border on the Mexican side. This sort of "third-party" deportation is illegal and, in the case of minors, constitutes child endangerment under American law. More importantly, it exposes people to extreme danger.

As a humanitarian and an opponent of all borders on principle, I will say that this sudden change in US Border Patrol policy was a step in the right direction, and even that it undoubtedly saved some lives. Needless to say, though, word got around about this, and large numbers of Central American minors started heading north, both with and without their mothers.

Meanwhile, in Mexico in early 2014, I saw firsthand that the Mexican authorities on the Guatemalan border were issuing seven-day transmigration forms to Central Americans en masse, including to busloads of single men. This is not normal behavior on the part of these authorities, either. When we started meeting many of these people in southern Arizona, it turned out that a great many of them were indigenous Mam speakers from the provinces of San Marcos and Huehuetenango in Guatemala, which are well known as areas of resource extraction. Then we started hearing different versions of a similar story: the cartels were trying to clear out parts of San Marcos and Huehuetenango along the Chiapas border, in order to use the territory for drug smuggling, human trafficking, and mining. I can't empirically prove this (and I'm not sure which tail was wagging which dog), but based on a large amount of anecdotal evidence, I feel confident that something fairly scandalous was happening. If this is true, it had to involve a coordination of policy on some level by the American, Mexican, and Guatemalan governments, by the major cartels, and by various mining companies—most likely Canadian.

The period ended later in 2014, after the "crisis" briefly became major news and the Border Patrol stopped releasing Central American minors and women with underage children. The Obama administration later deported many of the women and children who entered the country during this time, and the Trump administration will undoubtedly attempt to deport most of the rest.

Was this widely publicized crisis the result of a sincere effort to manage the border more compassionately? Was it a cold-blooded displacement strategy that directly benefited corporate, governmental, and criminal elites of four countries? Or was it both at once? I have no way to be certain. My guess is a little of the former and a lot of the latter. I wish an actual investigative journalist had tried to pin down what was happening; in fact, no one in any sector of the press put these pieces together.

Regardless, the episode illustrates one of my central themes. The regulation of human movement according to place of birth cannot be made just. Even well-intentioned attempts to enact humane border policies will have unforeseen and probably undesirable consequences.

"At the same moment a K-Line container filled with cheap shirts from Honduras enters the Hobart rail yard, ICE knocks down a door in South Gate and deports an entire family back to Tegucigalpa. To the south, the intermodal trains heading towards *El Norte* are alternately called *La Bestia* or *El Tren de la Muerte*—we think these names are apt. Commodity capital crosses into Southern California unscathed, but the fortunate family members and loved ones that survive harrowing journeys aboard the roofs of these trains for sometimes thousands of miles, must disembark—barred entry into the very same country that willingly accepts the commodities that some of the very same migrants produced with their own sweat and blood back in Centroamérica."

– *"How to Stop A Wound From Bleeding,"*
L.A. Onda

The Product

It is not possible to understand what happens next in the process of crossing the border without a lengthy tangent on the subject of . . . marijuana.

Capital

One of the strongest arguments in favor of the legalization of street drugs in the United States is that it would take some of the oxygen out of the Mexican drug war. (There are many other good arguments, but that's not my focus here.) This much is true. However, to understand the likely consequences of legalization, it's necessary to understand the North American drug market. It's particularly important to understand the marijuana market, since it's unlikely that other street drugs will be legalized any time soon.

Most high-grade marijuana consumed in the United States is grown domestically, especially in northern California. The industry is highly decentralized; there are thousands of independent operations in California and in many other states. Most low-grade marijuana consumed in the United States is grown in Mexico, in parts of Baja California and the Sierra Madre Occidental controlled by the Sinaloa Cartel. The industry is highly centralized; there is only one game in town.

The two industries have traditionally occupied separate market niches. Small- to mid-scale marijuana cultivation is legal, semi-legal, or tolerated in some parts of the United States. However, there is nowhere that it is possible to grow marijuana on the scale on which it is grown in Mexico. Even after marking up the price to move the product across the border, Sinaloa can still undersell American growers when dealing in bulk. Exporting the product means compacting it, though, which degrades the quality. So traditionally, Sinaloa has dealt with larger quantities of lower quality product, and American growers have dealt with smaller quantities of higher quality product.

This has begun to change. As legalization efforts in the United States have progressed, marijuana prices have dropped across the board. Sinaloa is still hanging on to its market share, but if it becomes possible to grow marijuana on an industrial scale in the United States, or even on a slightly larger scale than it is now, American growers will be able to cut Sinaloa out of the market. The obvious endgame of this is that a heavily subsidized American agribusiness company, probably a tobacco company, would *export* marijuana to Mexico, dominating that market as well, as Mexican growers could not hope to compete on such a scale. Wait, where have we heard this before?*

It is tempting to say "Good!" and leave it at that. Sinaloa is not a benign organization.

However, cutting it out of the American marijuana market will have unpleasant consequences. I respect some aspects of the marijuana legalization movement, but single-issue activists are deluding themselves if they think that legalization will only bring positive results.

Here is why.

As I described above, the two main camps in the Mexican drug war are organized under different business models, and use different marketing strategies. Sinaloa's camp controls the major migration and marijuana-smuggling routes along the border. It controls territory where marijuana and poppies are grown, so it can produce its own marijuana and heroin, along with every kind of drug that can be manufactured in a lab. It distributes every kind of drug in existence, both for domestic consumption and for export to the United States. Compared to the Zetas' camp, it profits more from these activities, and less from extortion, kidnapping, and contract killing.

---

* Something similar is happening in some parts of the United States where drug dealing is de facto the only means of livelihood. It's not good to put inner-city kids in jail for selling marijuana, but what happens if drug-dealing is taken away and there is nothing to replace it? Users will buy their product from the corporate dispensary rather than from the kids on the corner. What exactly will street-level drug dealers do?

The Zetas do not control major migration or marijuana-smuggling routes along the border. They do not control territory where marijuana or poppies are grown, so they cannot produce their own marijuana or heroin. They do produce every kind of drug that can be made in a lab. They distribute every kind of drug in existence, both for domestic consumption and for export to the United States—*except for marijuana*. The Zetas are not major players in the American marijuana market. It would make no sense; they could only buy from their competitors and they could never sell as cheaply.* They must import heroin for distribution, usually from Afghanistan. Compared to Sinaloa, they profit more from extortion, kidnapping, and murder-for-hire.

Of all of these activities, the only one that necessitates upholding one end of a social contract is the cultivation of marijuana and poppies: to grow crops, Sinaloa must deal with the campesinos that work the fields. Sinaloa demands obedience, and in return it promises to protect and care for its people. In this way, it is no different from any other government—effectively, it *is* the government. In the territory that Sinoloa governs, it largely upholds its end of the bargain. Sinaloa has an interest in social stability; the Zetas have an interest in social instability.

For all of these reasons, marijuana legalization affects Sinaloa more than the Zetas. However, the drop in prices is not hurting Sinaloa's bottom line. The organization is robust. It has a diverse portfolio and various contingency plans. At the moment, it also has to uphold its end of the social contract. So the drop in marijuana prices has led Sinaloa to shift production to poppies in the Sierra Madre Occidental. This led first to a drop in heroin prices in the United States, then to a spike in demand, and then to a dramatic increase in heroin overdoses nationwide. This is the origin of the heroin 'epidemic' that the American press began to report on in 2014.† Even if the Mexican marijuana industry collapses

* The Zetas certainly grow and sell *some* marijuana. The point is that they don't do so at anything approaching the scale that Sinaloa does.

† The heroin epidemic is itself part of the broader opioid epidemic that began around 2005, stemming from the over-prescription of legal painkillers.

completely, it will probably not cost Sinaloa one cent. Sinoloa will increase heroin production until there is no more room to grow poppies, or until the American market is so saturated that it can absorb no more production. Given the nature of heroin, this might be hard to do.[‡]

If marijuana collapsed and heroin simultaneously reached saturation, then some part of Sinaloa's agrarian base would become expendable, and would be abandoned. Sinaloa could then fall back on cocaine and lab drugs, but most likely there would eventually be some breakdown in distribution or logistics. Only after all of this happens would the legalization of marijuana actually begin to cost Sinaloa money. If Sinaloa starts to lose money, that distinctly favors the Zetas. This is not what most marijuana legalization activists are hoping for.

At the moment, marijuana is a special case; an actual end to drug prohibition in the United States is not in the cards. However, social attitudes are changing, and it's worth speculating about what effects the end of prohibition would have in Mexico.

An end to prohibition would spell trouble for all the cartels. Prices would drop, which would cause a spike in demand, which would call for more supply. Eventually, the market would be glutted to the point that profits would diminish, and the only solution would be to rely on an economy of scale to reduce costs. This has already happened with marijuana.

Faced with diminishing profits, the cartels would not just ride off into the sunset. They would look for other sources of revenue, such as extortion, kidnapping, and contract killing. Failing all of this, if the cartels did go under, the lower-ranking members would be thrown out of work first. It would move up the food chain and affect the biggest fish last.

---

‡ The damage that the drug industry inflicts on users is not the focus of this book, but I am well aware of the toll it takes. I have friends who have died from using heroin, most likely Sinaloan. For a practical, radical, and compassionate perspective on addiction, see *In the Realm of Hungry Ghosts* by Dr. Gabor Maté.

The cartels are *employers.* Like it or not, they provide a source of income to many people. Simply "putting them out of business" would leave large numbers of people with no clear means of subsistence. To be precise, it would do that *unless it was accompanied by a wider social transformation that enabled them to pursue another way of life.*

So what am I advocating? I am not dismissing activists' efforts to decriminalize the use and sale of marijuana. It's a step in the right direction, and it has helped shift the grounds of debate. But let there be no illusions: marijuana legalization, minus an end to drug prohibition, will bring a new set of problems. And barring broader social change, the end of drug prohibition would bring another.

Labor

Most hard drugs are smuggled into the United States in vehicles, through every official port of entry along the entire border. As often as not, this is accomplished with the assistance of corrupt Custom and Border Protection Agents working the ports. All that the agent needs to know is what vehicle to look for so as to wave it through instead of stopping it, and the job is done. Much of the Mexican drug war boils down to conflict over who controls these ports of entry.

Marijuana is different. Being cheap, bulky, and fragrant,* it is mostly carried through the desert on foot. This is accomplished by groups of *burros* ("donkeys")† who carry the fifty-pound bales of highly compacted marijuana on their backs. This is not an

* Much like the author of this text!

† This term is used widely. Someone a little higher in the pecking order of these groups is likely to be called a *"burrero,"* or "donkey-herder." Neither English nor Spanish provides any term to refer to these people that is simultaneously neutral, standard, and not derogatory. Lacking any alternative, I'll very begrudgingly alternate between "burro," since that's what absolutely everybody says in Spanish, and "marijuana smuggler," since that sounds normal in English and is as close to neutral as anything else I can think of.

easy task. The desert consumes these people just as readily as migrants and refugees, and to the mafias that employ them they are indeed as expendable as donkeys.

There are two basic kinds of marijuana smugglers. The first, mostly from northern Sonora, are those who do it for a living. They might start working when they are barely teenagers, and some of them know the desert better than any Border Patrol agent, even better than I do. They are paid about as well as public-school teachers in the United States, which is to say much better than employees in any other line of work available to most young men from northern Sonora. It's a job.‡

The second, mostly from Central America, are those who do it one time. These people are in fact migrants or refugees. Instead of paying the mafia thousands of dollars to get into the United States, they pay for their passage by carrying a bale. The bale might be worth $100,000. The burro takes all the risk and gets paid nothing, but for Central Americans with little or no money, it's the best deal in town. Sometimes this risk is not freely chosen, either. It's not unheard of for travelers (usually Central American) to be kidnapped at the border and press-ganged into service.

Those who transport marijuana for a living can often be found in groups with those who are doing it just once. It's common for a group to consist of six to eight Hondurans, who carry the weight, and one or two Sonorans to lead the way.

When spoken to like normal human beings, these people tend to be as quick as anyone else to tell their side of the story. It often sounds a lot like this:

‡ "I've been working this fucking job since I was twelve," one young man told me. He said he was nineteen. "It takes me ten days going north and four days going south. I rest for a couple of days at my mom's house and do it again. I make two trips a month, they pay me a thousand bucks a trip. I've been beaten, robbed, stabbed, shot, and just about died in the desert more times than I can fucking remember. All my old friends are either dead or in jail in the United States. I'm sick of this shit. This is my last run, I swear to god. I'm gonna open up a tire shop in Los Angeles and send money back home to my mom." Hollywood has nothing on these guys. They look like grown men by the time they're sixteen; by the time they're thirty, they look like Aragorn.

Border Patrol apprehends a group. One of three things happens. Sometimes they confiscate the marijuana, then detain and prosecute the group for drug smuggling. There are Border Patrol agents who are not in on the game. Besides, it wouldn't look right if no marijuana ever showed up in court. Other times, they confiscate the marijuana, then detain and deport the group *as migrants*. In this case, the marijuana never shows up in court. Is the burro going to say anything to the judge? No. And still other times, they confiscate the marijuana and just leave the group in the desert to walk back to Mexico.*

I've heard this all over and over again. Multiple unconnected people are not making up the same story. What could be happening? Onto whom could these agents be unloading all of this marijuana? Who can possibly deal with 500 pounds at once? There is only one answer: Sinaloa.

Burros and their loads are traded as favors, passed around in complex horse-trading between law enforcement and organized crime. The mafia understands that agents on the take have to keep up appearances, and that a percentage of the product will be lost. Agents on the take understand that the mafia has to move enough product to keep the wheels turning, and that it's not in anyone's interest to actually shut the sector down. Everybody wins, except for the kid from Honduras who has to sit in prison when it's his turn to take the fall.

Once, a Sonoran teenager asked me how much Border Patrol agents in the field get paid. I told him that a normal salary was about $70,000. He thought that was hilarious. "They can get more than double that any time they feel like taking one of our loads. They only have to do it once or twice a year and they're set. We do all the hard work for them."

Government bodies sometimes claim that solidarity workers such as ourselves are aiding and abetting drug traffickers. This is the height of irony and hypocrisy. Elements of Border Patrol and Customs and Border Protection are engaged in drug trafficking

---

* "Ugh, this sucks," the haggard guy with the gold tooth told me. "Border Patrol just took all our weed and told us to fuck off."

on an industrial scale. This is not an accusation; it is a statement of fact. Any but the greenest BP or CBP agent knows it's true. If anyone within these agencies is actually interested in fighting a war on drugs, they should start by cleaning their own house.

And for the record: no, I've never seen a bale. The entire job description of a burro is to make sure that doesn't happen. I don't think anyone deserves to die in the desert for carrying marijuana, and I have no legal obligation to ask a starved and dehydrated person what he does for a living before I give him food or water. Also, if Americans don't like marijuana smugglers, they shouldn't smoke so much marijuana. I don't smoke any myself.

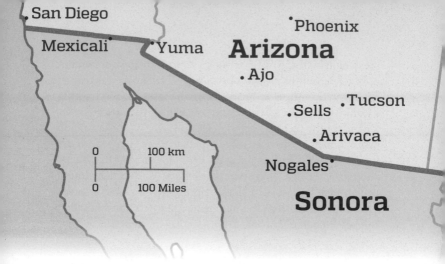

The Border

As a physical space, you could visualize the US-Mexico border as a zone demarcated by three lines of control, extending east-to-west from Brownsville-Matamoros to San Diego-Tijuana. The southern line, usually well inside of Mexico, is wherever it becomes necessary to pay someone to pass. There is not one inch of the border that is not spoken for by somebody. Even crossing without a guide means paying a large fee to whatever combination of mafia and the government patrols the southern side. It is not advisable to attempt to avoid paying this fee.*

The central line is the international boundary. The northern line, 25 to 50 miles inside of the United States, is at the interior

---

* I once met a Honduran who did manage to get around this by waiting in Nogales for weeks until the night of a much-anticipated boxing match. "I knew that every one of those fuckers was going to be watching Manny Pacquiao," he told me. "I waited for the fight to start and I snuck past them while they were in front of the TV."

checkpoints. These are places where Border Patrol stops and inspects all vehicles on all major roads. They profile passengers based on skin color first and English fluency second. Anyone who looks brown is going to have to demonstrate good English. Some people without papers who look brown and speak English well can bluff their way through. However, anyone who looks brown and doesn't speak English well is going to get asked for papers. Anyone who looks brown, doesn't speak English well, and doesn't have papers is going to get taken in.

So, to cross the border, you have to be granted passage through the southern line, cross the boundary line, and then get all the way past the northern line to a place where it's possible to be driven to safety in a vehicle.

In some cities and towns, the southern line collapses onto the central line at the border wall. This occurs in places where it's impossible to cross the international boundary. So you don't have to pay anyone off to get to the city of Nogales, but you can't cross the wall there, either. If you want to get out into the desert where you can cross the boundary line, somebody has to be paid. The northern line extends the whole length of the United States. It's never easy and usually very difficult to get away from the border on the American side without driving through a checkpoint.

There are two main sets of migration routes. The northwestern routes are in Sonora and are controlled by the Sinaloa Cartel. These are also the main routes for overland marijuana smuggling. The northeastern routes are in Tamaulipas, and controlled by the Gulf Cartel. The latter is a former rival and current ally of Sinaloa, and appears to be doing business on a similar model. In Sonora, the business of human trafficking and marijuana smuggling is so closely interlinked that it is simplest to discuss it as a single operation.

The two main sets of routes share those basic characteristics, but are otherwise completely different. The northwestern routes traverse basin-and-range topography, picturesquely described by Clarence Dutton as "an army of caterpillars marching toward Mexico." These routes change elevation abruptly as they alternate between rugged mountain ranges and arid basins. It is usually bone-dry; the winters are quite cold, and in the summer it is a blazing furnace. The entire space between the southern and northern lines of control is wild and uninhabited desert. Most of the American side is public, tribal, or military land.

The northeastern routes traverse flat, sandy scrublands. It is usually very humid, and in the summer it is swelteringly hot. The central line of control is the Rio Grande; it passes through the metropolitan areas of the river valley. Huge cattle ranches occupy the space between the central and northern lines. Nearly all of the American side is private land.

There is no need to describe every migration corridor in the country in detail. People cross everywhere. However, it's worth spending some time on the places where the most deaths occur: southern Arizona and south Texas.

The most heavily traveled part of Arizona can be broken into three subcategories. The eastern routes, traversing a hodgepodge of public land jurisdictions, are between the Atascosa Mountains and the Baboquivari Mountains. They are at a slightly higher elevation and are slightly cooler, but they also feature the most rugged and confusing terrain. It's very easy to get lost. These places are extremely sparsely inhabited; there are far more deer and cows than people. The only place between the boundary line and the northern line of control where anyone lives is the town of Arivaca. This is where our solidarity work has been focused for many years.

The central routes through Arizona, which traverse Tohono O'odham tribal land, pass between the Baboquivari Mountains and the Ajo Mountains. They are hotter and at a lower elevation than those around Arivaca. There are areas of the reservation that are uninhabited, but there are also many places where people live. For many years, we didn't work on the reservation. Over the last several years, we have been doing occasional search and rescue operations there, under specific circumstances and with permission from the tribal government.

The western routes pass between the Ajo Mountains and the Mohawk Mountains across a mixture of public and military land.

They are lower, hotter, and even more sparsely inhabited than anywhere else. The only place where anyone lives is the town of Ajo. We started working in this area several years ago.

The busiest part of Texas is in Brooks County, between McAllen and Falfurrias.

Let's look at each of these places in detail.

Arivaca

The unlikely story of how Arivaca came to be an epicenter of efforts in solidarity with migrants and refugees is both interesting and instructive.

Arivaca, AZ is an unincorporated community of about 700 people. The population is widely dispersed across many small to medium-sized ranches. There is one bar, one store, and anywhere from three to six churches depending on the season. Maybe it would be possible to break down the racial demographics between Anglos and Latinos, or the subcultural demographics between cowboys and hippies, but Arivacans have been miscegenating in every way for so long that most of them are something in between. The place is actually wild. There is still buckshot in the doorway of the bar, where a man named Lucky accidently blew off his arm with a sawed-off shotgun that he had stuck in his coat. No one seems to believe that Lucky had any particularly bad intentions; that was just how he rolled.

Arivaca became ground zero for everything related to migration and border militarization in the years after the attacks of September 11, 2001. Border Patrol pushed traffic west out of Nogales and forced it into the remote desert surrounding Arivaca. Thousands of travelers started turning up at Arivacans' back doors in every imaginable stage of desperation. Before long, Arivaca itself became heavily militarized; caravans of Border Patrol would roll through town at all hours of day and night, loaded for bear and generally treating the place as if it were Iraq. No More Deaths began to work in Arivaca in 2004.

Arivaca briefly made national news in 2009. This story has been told and retold.* What happened afterwards is less widely known. On May 30, two white supremacists from the Pacific northwest (Shawna Forde and Jason Bush), an Arivaca man (Albert Gaxiola), and a never-identified fourth party committed double-murder at the Arivaca home of Raul "Junior" Flores, his wife Gina Gonzalez, their eleven-year-old daughter Alexandra Flores, and their nine-year-old daughter Brisenia Flores.

Forde and Bush had been bouncing around the white supremacist and border vigilante milieu for years. Forde was an affiliate of Chris Simcox, the nationally-known founder and spokesman of a succession of "Minuteman" militia groups. She had concocted a plan to rob "cartel members" in order to fund a new group, Minutemen American Defense. She enlisted the assistance of Bush, who was associated with the Aryan Brotherhood, and who is suspected to have committed two additional racially motivated murders in the state of Washington in 1997.† Gaxiola led them to the Flores home.

Junior Flores, by most accounts I've heard around town, was probably involved on some level in the local marijuana business—like a fair number of other people in southern Arizona. He is generally thought to have run afoul of Gaxiola, who was also involved, because of something related to this. Flores may not have been a completely law-abiding citizen, but most people seem to agree that calling him a "cartel member" was a pretty serious stretch. Nobody thinks that he deserved what happened next. In the news, if not in Arivaca, it was usually mentioned

* See *And Hell Followed With Her* by David Neiwert.
† In the first case, a witness says that he was walking with Bush late the night of July 24, that they came upon a homeless man sleeping on the ground, and that Bush stabbed him to death. The victim was later identified as Hector Lopez Partida. The witness says that he attended an Aryan Nations gathering in northern Idaho with Bush three days later, and that they both wore yellow laces in their boots as a symbol of having killed someone. In the second case, a witness says that Bush executed a fellow white supremacist named Jon Bumstead two months later, because he was "a traitor to the race and a Jew."

that both Flores and Gonzalez were third-generation citizens of the United States.

Forde, Bush, and Gaxiola woke the Flores family out of their sleep around 5 am; dressed in camouflage, wearing bulletproof vests, and claiming to be Border Patrol. Alexandra was sleeping away from home. When Flores asked them for identification, Bush shot him in the chest and shot Gonzalez in the leg. They ransacked the house but failed to find anything of value. Bush then shot Brisenia in the head. Gonzalez was able to return fire, wounding Bush, and the assailants fled. She survived, and told and retold the story about the people who barged into her house in the middle of the night and murdered her husband and daughter for no reason.

When this all came to light, it sent the border vigilante movement into a tailspin from which it has never recovered, and probably never will. It has since disemboweled itself. In April 2010, Chris Simcox's wife was granted a protection order after he allegedly brandished a gun at her and threatened to shoot her and their children. In June 2013, he was arrested on multiple counts related to child molestation and sexual conduct with a minor, involving three girls under the age of 10, one of whom is his daughter; Simcox was convicted of child sexual abuse in June 2016 and is serving a prison sentence of nineteen and a half years. In May 2012, another Arizona border vigilante leader, Jason "JT" Ready, shot and killed his girlfriend, her daughter, her daughter's fiancee, and her 15-month-old granddaughter before turning the gun on himself. The "Minutemen" have shown themselves for what they are: people looking for opportunities to inflict violence down the social hierarchy, often on children.

Albert Gaxiola was sentenced to life in prison plus an additional seventy-two years. Shawna Forde and Jason Bush are on death row, looking for supporters. They have found none. Gina Gonzalez, at terrible cost, can go to her grave knowing that she fired the shots that sent this odious milieu to hell. God only knows what would have happened if her aim had been less true.

It's almost impossible to overstate the impact of the Flores murders in Arivaca. Everyone knew Gina and Junior; everyone's kids went to school with Brisenia. I was in Arivaca on the day of the killings and remained there for months afterwards. The mood in the bar was not just sorrowful, but ominous. I thought that there would be retribution.

After the murders, solidarity workers like us were the only game left in town. It was clear that there was a crisis; no one could ignore it. The crisis would come to you, in the form of a desperate Honduran woman knocking on your window in the middle of the night. The state had discredited itself completely by bringing on this crisis and then by treating Arivaca like a war zone. The vigilantes had proven themselves to be child-murderers. We had been there for five years, leaving water bottles in the desert. It was pretty clear whose side to take.

As of 2016, there is a humanitarian aid office across the street from the bar, there have been repeated protests and acts of civil disobedience at the Border Patrol checkpoint outside of town, and there is often a big sign that says "Militias Go Home" on display when you drive into the tiny Sunday farmers' market. I doubt that there is any municipality in the entire country where a higher percentage of people have acted concretely in solidarity with migrants and refugees, or where a lower percentage of people will cooperate with Border Patrol if they can possibly avoid it.

Solidarity workers from other places have contributed to this, but we did not lead, and people from Arivaca did not follow. If anything, the inverse was true. Locals had been helping people for years before we got there. What happened was a two-way street; locals and outsiders influenced each other. At this point, it's becoming difficult to tell the difference between the two.

Neither the state nor the vigilantes have any hope of regaining the sympathies of this town. You can't put people under siege and expect them to forget. Nor can you shoot a nine-year-old girl in the face and expect to be forgiven. At this point, when people in Arivaca run into travelers in need of assistance, they are most likely to deal with it themselves, or to reach out to us for help. They are not very likely to call Border Patrol. Not in a thousand years will anyone call the vigilantes.

Komkch'ed e Wah 'osithk (Sells)

The politics of migration on the Tohono O'odham reservation are extremely complex. I am not O'odham, and I don't speak for any O'odham people. Some O'odham thinkers whose analyses have been useful to me personally include Ofelia Rivas, Alex Soto, and Mike Wilson. I encourage the reader to seek out their commentary, while understanding that O'odham opinions differ widely and sometimes directly clash.

This is what I can say from my vantage point.

To reiterate this, European colonists stole the land that currently makes up the border between Arizona and Sonora from its original inhabitants by means of genocide. It is O'odham, Apache, and Yaqui land, occupied by the governments of Mexico and the United States.* If anyone has a right to decide who can pass through O'odham territory, it is O'odham people, not either of those governments.

There are many indigenous communities in the United States, and many southern border communities as well, but the Tohono O'odham reservation is one of the only places in the country that is truly both. That means that it not only gets the problems of Arivaca, but of Pine Ridge to boot.† It's no exaggeration to say that it has been converted into a militarized police state. O'odham people are subject to rampant harassment and racial profiling on their own land, pulled out of their cars and houses left and right by Border Patrol agents fresh out of Connecticut who can't tell red from brown and couldn't tell

---

* See the O'Odham Declaration of Allegiance to Mother Earth, O'Odham Voice Against the Wall, October 2011.

† See Peter Matthiessen's *In the Spirit of Crazy Horse* for more on Pine Ridge. There are also Lipan Apache, Yoeme, and Kickapoo communities on the southern border, though they are physically much smaller than the Tohono O'odham reservation.

you the difference between Sells, Arizona and San Pedro Sula, Honduras. The border has sundered O'odham on the south side from their relatives on the north; militarization and migration have led to the desecration of sacred sites and the disruption of ceremonies. In addition, O'odham people face the same problems as many other indigenous people in the United States: poverty, unemployment, erosion of cultural identity, multigenerational trauma, and more.

The federal government has gone out of its way to push traffic onto the Tohono O'odham reservation, out of the sight of white people. Almost every year, more people die there than on any other comparably-sized section of the entire border. The government has offered up the reservation as a sacrifice zone to the border militarization, drug smuggling, and human trafficking industries, in the same way that it has offered up Black Mesa to the coal industry and Yucca Mountain to the nuclear industry—to name just two of countless examples. In all these cases, it has found tribal "leaders" willing to play ball. They have turned the O'odham *jewed* (homeland) into a deathtrap.

The O'odham tribal government works closely with Border Patrol, and forbids humanitarian aid on the reservation, taking the position that such aid would encourage more migration through O'odham land. In my opinion, this position is asinine; it is clearly the actions of the federal government that have pushed the traffic onto O'odham land and ensure that it will stay there. I do, however, recognize that the federal government has put the tribal government in an impossible position; they're damned if they do and damned if they don't. They can control what the humanitarian aid organizations do, but they can't control what Border Patrol does. I also recognize that the tribal government is not a monolithic entity; there are dissenting voices within it.

More importantly, there is no shortage of O'odham people acting autonomously of the tribal government. O'odham people have been at the forefront of many of the more interesting things happening in Arizona in recent years—from the May 2010 occupation of the Border Patrol headquarters in Tucson to the December 2011 actions to disrupt the American Legislative

Exchange Council (ALEC) conference in Scottsdale, the ongoing campaign against the 202 Loop outside of Phoenix, and many other examples. I've heard countless stories of O'odham people acting in solidarity with travelers passing through their land.

As usual, there is no easy solution. There is no simple reform that will end the suffering on the reservation. I think it's fair to say that most O'odham people are well aware of the terrible irony that thousands of people, including a great number of indigenous people, are dying on their homeland. I seriously doubt that many O'odham are happy about this.

In my opinion, it would be a step in the right direction if the tribal government would allow humanitarian aid organizations to operate on the reservation. But if that were the only thing to change, if the federal government were allowed to continue to use the reservation as a sacrifice zone, then yes, it's possible that this would only lead to more traffic on O'odham land. The needs of undocumented people cannot be untangled from the needs of indigenous people.

Ajo

This place is grim. Rocky, barren, devoid of shade, and fearsomely, ferociously hot.

Some of this territory was the site of the incident of May 2001 described in *The Devil's Highway* by Luís Alberto Urrea, when 14 people died here trying to cross near the Growler Mountains. Despite the fact that the author credulously accepts a lot of Border Patrol public relations talking points at face value, that book did draw a lot of attention to the deaths on the border.

Land jurisdiction on these routes is divided between Organ Pipe National Monument, Cabeza Prieta National Wildlife Reserve, Bureau of Land Management, and the Barry M. Goldwater Air Force Range. Public access to Cabeza Prieta and especially the Barry Goldwater range is strictly controlled. Outside of the town of Ajo, absolutely no one lives on these routes. Many routes miss Ajo entirely. Tourists do frequent Organ Pipe. Very few civilians ever set foot on Cabeza Prieta, and fewer still on the Barry Goldwater.

When we began to work in this area, we noticed something suspicious: every year lots of human remains are discovered in Organ Pipe, but almost none in Cabeza Prieta or on the Barry Goldwater. This doesn't mean people aren't dying there—it just means nobody ever goes there to find out. When we started going into Cabeza Prieta and onto the Barry Goldwater, we started finding remains immediately.

In addition to all the challenges I've already described, people who cross the Barry Goldwater have to contend with the fact that it's an active bombing range full of unexploded ordinance. It's possible to be blown up from above or from below. Nobody has any idea how frequently this happens. There are areas where even Border Patrol can't go.

Picture this:

There is a place inside the bombing range. It exists. We've heard about it more than once, but we don't know exactly where it is. It's a facsimile of a town that the Air Force has built to practice bombing. They build and destroy it perpetually. Unless people know better, they head toward this place, thinking that surely they must be in sight of *something*, maybe even Gila Bend. What they find is that they have wandered into the set of a movie about Stalingrad, featuring real bombs and no direction from above.

This is probably the worst place on the entire border.

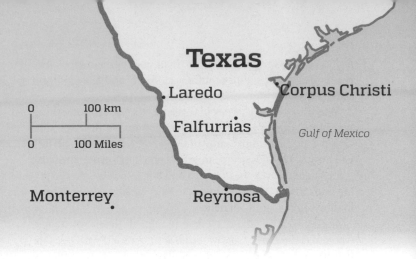

Falfurrias

Brooks County, in rural southern Texas, is listed as the poorest county in the state and regularly makes the list of poorest counties in the entire country. It has recently seen an explosion of migrant deaths, especially of Central Americans. As in Arizona, large numbers of people are dying while trying to circumvent the Falfurrias checkpoint on Highway 281.

Since 2012, there have been some months when more remains have been discovered in Brooks County than on any part of the Tohono O'odham reservation of comparable size. This was previously unheard of. I am less conversant with the situation in Tamaulipas and Texas than I am with Sonora and Arizona, but I am fairly sure that I can pinpoint three basic reasons why this happened.

The first is because of border militarization in Arizona. This is usually the first factor mentioned in the American press. I believe this has had a role, but not as much as is often portrayed. In my experience, militarization in Arizona mostly serves to move traffic around Arizona itself—from one trail to another, from Arivaca to the reservation, from the reservation to Ajo, and so on. However, it is true that it's more difficult to cross there now than it was in the late 2000s. I don't doubt that some people have decided to take their chances with Texas instead.

The second reason that is usually mentioned is the Border Patrol's policy change, in effect from late 2013 until some time in 2014. As I mentioned earlier, during this time, they were not immediately deporting unaccompanied Central American minors or Central American mothers with underage children. Word did get around. I was in Guatemala in early 2014, and there were fliers hanging up on telephone poles everywhere, saying things like, "*Señoras*! It is I, Roberto, your humble and honest servant! I swear before God that I can get you and your children into the United States! No hiding in a tractor-trailer truck! No walking in the desert! Call me at any time of day or night: 5867-5309!" However, this doesn't explain everything. After all, the Border Patrol never stopped deporting Central American men, or women without children, and these demographics have been well represented in south Texas as well. Many if not most of the unaccompanied minors and women with underage children who crossed into south Texas during this time didn't try to circumvent the checkpoint; they crossed the international boundary and then sought out Border Patrol to turn themselves in. This is a very different thing, and much less dangerous.

The third reason, rarely mentioned in the American press, is cartel politics on the Mexican side. The onset of the Brooks County deaths generally coincided with a series of setbacks to the Zetas. Several influential Zetas leaders were killed or captured around this time (October 2012 to October 2013), and the Gulf Cartel won back control of Reynosa, where they had been battling with the Zetas for several years. Lo and behold, shortly afterwards, large numbers of Central Americans started turning up in Brooks County. It appears to me that the Gulf Cartel put out the word in Central America: "OK, the adults are back in charge. You can come this way again. Call Roberto." It appears to me that there was a period after the San Fernando massacres where the human trafficking business in Tamaulipas all but broke down. Now it's business as usual, which means that people are going to die.

This has created a perfect storm in south Texas.

South Texas is clearly calling out for solidarity efforts. The situation there is bad. A lot of people are dying. It would be great if a campaign in solidarity with migrants and refugees took place there on a scale comparable to the one in Arizona. However, this has proven difficult. What happened in Arizona was an organic outgrowth of a particular set of conditions. It can't just be exported to Texas.

For starters, there are two fundamental differences between south Texas and southern Arizona. First, a lot of the land on which people are dying in Arizona is public, so we can operate on it freely. Practically all the land on which people are dying in south Texas is private. So operating on it means getting the consent if not the participation of the owners and workers on large cattle ranches. This is possible, but it takes work.*

The second difference is that, while southern Arizona is extremely mountainous, south Texas is completely flat. Mountains create trails, which make for lots of good places to drop supplies. In flat places, there's nothing to force people to walk one place instead of another. The best that can be done is to haul fifty-gallon drums of water to various places, put blue flags on them, and hope people see them. Again, this isn't impossible, but it necessitates the participation and consent of private landowners.

The last complicating factor is that while it was radicals who got on the ground first in Arizona, in Texas it was not. Lacking other options to respond to the large number of deaths, Brooks County ranchers began organizing their own patrols to look for

* It is not the case that ranchers and ranch hands are automatically hostile to migrants, or even to solidarity workers and their radical politics. Sometimes they are, but not always. In fact, this is precisely our base of support in Arivaca, which is why our organization is robust and will not be dislodged from there any time soon. For one thing, a lot of ranchers and especially ranch hands are Latino. For another, even people who might otherwise be right-wing tend to soften up when they have to look death and suffering in the face. In Arizona there is an *inverse* relationship between the "average" white person's level of empathy for migrants and the distance from the border. Arivaca is extremely sympathetic; Phoenix is extremely hostile.

people. They would patrol each other's ranches, look for people in distress, and call Border Patrol when they found them. It appears to me to that this was mostly an organic response to the crisis, later influenced somewhat by reactionary activists of the national border vigilante milieu. As mentioned before, this milieu has been completely discredited in Arizona. Honestly, the civilian patrols were probably better than nothing. They almost certainly saved lives.

However, collaborating with Border Patrol in this way is something that we adamantly don't do in Arizona. We never help them apprehend people, and we never turn anybody in unless they ask us to. Maintaining an adversarial relationship with Border Patrol has helped us to curb migrant deaths, not hindered us. Being clear about our politics has allowed us to seek support in the right places, and has given us credibility where we need it. On a practical level, it means that people who need help don't have to hide from us. It has also allowed us to "good-cop/bad-cop" Border Patrol when we need to negotiate. This dynamic in south Texas has been exacerbated by the fact that, if anything, Border Patrol has been better behaved there than in Arizona. Border Patrol *is* the problem; it can't be part of the solution. Not even if individual agents or sector chiefs try, which occasionally they do.

All of that said, there are a variety of groups and individuals doing effective work in Brooks County, notably the South Texas Human Rights Center in Falfurrias. If the reader wants to get involved or initiate a new project, I encourage you to contact somebody there or in Corpus Christi.

Two ranchers lived near us: *El Pelón* and Crazy Mark. Both Vietnam veterans, they were a study in contrasts.

El Pelón was as bald as a cue ball, and wore a magnificent Ho Chi Minh mustache—"a worthy adversary," he told me, describing the Vietnamese communist leader. He had seen heavy combat in the Marine Corps, and had repeatedly been exposed to Agent Orange. He had moved to the desert after the war, and had been helping migrants in distress since long before No More Deaths or any other humanitarian aid organization arrived. He gave food and water to thousands of people over the years. He liked us. I used to feed his donkeys.

Crazy Mark hated us with a passion. He would destroy our water bottles whenever he could find them, and occasionally he would let off a couple of shots in the general direction of our camp. He made it clear to me on more than one occasion that he would be just as happy to put a hot one through my head. He would go around all the time in full camouflage and reflective sunglasses. He was really damaged and actually dangerous. People were afraid of him, and justifiably so. Everyone called him Crazy Mark behind his back, although never to his face. Everyone except *El Pelón*.

The two ranchers were close friends. *El Pelón* would frequently invite us over for dinner, to use his shower, or to get ice. Sometimes Crazy Mark would be there. One time he began to threaten me and one of my colleagues in lurid detail. *El Pelón* interrupted him. "These people are my guests, Mark. They are *under my protection.*"

El Pelón's health declined precipitously. We were spending a lot of time with him. He had flashbacks and all types of nerve damage. He never slept. He wouldn't eat or drink anything except coffee, and he would stay up all night watching war movies, chain-smoking and ashing on the floor. He was taking enough morphine and Oxycontin to drop a horse. We started sleeping up at his house as often as not.

One night there was a ferocious storm brewing. It was clear that it was going to rain harder than hell. It was cold. A group of seven migrants came knocking on the door.

"I'm sorry *señor,*" one of them said to *El Pelón*. "It's going to rain. Is there anywhere we can spend the night?"

"Yeah," *El Pelón* told him. "Get in the barn. It's warm and dry. There's plenty of straw." We went to sleep. It poured all night, with wind and thunder and lightning.

First thing in the morning we went out to look for anybody that had gotten caught in the storm. We didn't find anyone, and we went back to the house around noon, to check on the migrants. Another volunteer was in the driveway.

"*El Pelón* is dead," he told me. "He's in there in his bed. His dogs are freaking out. I did CPR and everything, but it's no use. I called 911 almost an hour ago. They should be out here any time." As soon as he had said this we saw an ambulance and a police car in the distance, bumping up the long and rocky road toward the house. My stomach dropped.

First, there were still seven migrants in the barn. Second, I was acutely aware of the fact that *El Pelón's* house was bursting at the seams with every kind of firearm imaginable, from ancient blunderbusses to 50-caliber machine guns and everything in between. There were a lot of ways that this could end badly. All of a sudden Crazy Mark came roaring up next to us on his four wheeler, seemingly out of nowhere. He wasn't wearing his sunglasses.

"Where is *El Pelón?!*" He sounded hoarse.

I dropped my head. "*El Pelón* is dead, Mark. I'm sorry."

We looked at each other. I drew a circle in the dirt with my foot. "This is me." I drew another circle, that touched the first one at only one point. "This is you." I twisted my foot on the point where the circles met. "This is *El Pelón*. Even if you and I don't have a single other thing in common we both loved him." My colleague ran to the barn, to tell the migrants to stay hidden in the straw. Mark left.

The paramedics drove off with *El Pelón's* body. The sheriff and the coroner followed them. The migrants left. Mark came back.

"We have to deal with the guns," he told me.

He disassembled each weapon methodically, one by one. "This one is OK. This one is OK. This one is a problem." The next day a lawyer came out to the house. All of the guns were disposed of legally.

The next time I saw Mark was at the memorial service, in front of the house. He had his sunglasses on. At the end of the service he did the three-volley salute with a pistol, for *El Pelón*. *Ready. Aim. Fire. Boom. Aim. Fire. Boom. Aim. Fire. Boom.* He didn't speak a word to me.

The war in Vietnam ended before I was born, but it killed my friend *El Pelón* just the same. The last thing he ever did was shelter seven people in his barn.

Mark stopped slashing our bottles. I never saw him again.

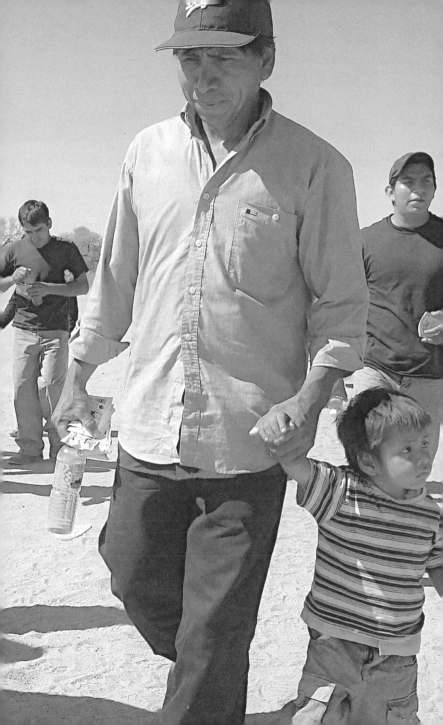

The Crossing

Now that I've set out some of the context, I'll summarize how the crossing goes in Sonora. I doubt it's much different in Tamaulipas.

People arrive in Altar (or Matamoros, Reynosa, Agua Prieta, Nogales, Caborca, Sonoyta, Mexicali...) and the mafias divide them up into groups. Groups of seven to fifteen people are pretty common. There are often two guides.

Sometimes, as I said, the mafia will send the migrants and the marijuana down the same routes. There are advantages to this: it allows them to use groups as diversions. Migrants might be a diversion for marijuana, or a smaller group might be a diversion for a larger one. The mafia has a million tricks; they're good at this. They'll hand Border Patrol a group today for a favor tomorrow. There's always a possibility that any particular group may be set up for a fall.

There are also times when they keep the groups separate. Marijuana is sent into more rugged routes, migrants into less rugged ones. This is the best-case scenario. However the traffic is organized, someone has to keep an eye on the big picture. There might be nine different groups heading out from Altar on any given day, with various others at different stages in the field. Somebody has to make sure all these people aren't tripping over each other, or that if they are it's for some purpose.

And they're off.

What happens next could be portrayed by a simple flow chart. Once a person sets out, there are three possible outcomes: arrival, deportation, or death. In the event of arrival, the person remains always at risk of being deported. In the event of deportation, the person may choose to try again. The cycle continues.

Every single story is different. But nearly all share similar themes.

The group starts walking well inside Mexico. They reach the area of the boundary line. Border Patrol focuses enforcement here; this is a risky time. If nothing goes wrong, the group crosses through and continues north. Some days later, if nothing goes wrong, they reach the northern line of control. Border Patrol focuses enforcement here as well; this is another risky time. If nothing goes wrong, they meet their ride, and are driven to a house or ranch somewhere. They are then either held for ransom or transported onward to their destination. Do they arrive? Hopefully.

As often as not, something does go wrong in the desert. The traveler is detained by Border Patrol or loses the guide. If travelers are detained, they are deported, or imprisoned and then deported. If they are separated from the guide, it is usually for one of two reasons. The first is that the guide abandons them because they are unable to keep up; they are sick, hurt, or out of shape. The second is that the guide loses them, usually because Border Patrol scattered the group. If they lose their guide, they are lost in the endless desert. They either find someone or they die. If they find a sympathetic person, they may still make it, if they are lucky. If they find Border Patrol, they will be detained. The cycle continues.

The border is designed to kill people. The system is not broken: it works.

Over the last few years, we have finally started to see travelers carrying cell phones with American service; these can be found on sale for about ten times their normal price in Altar and other origin points along the border. This means that when people end up in danger, they can call 911 like anybody else—provided that service is available, which varies greatly depending on the sector but is often not the case, a state of affairs that is itself no coincidence.

And where there is service, there is still the small matter that not all emergencies are created equal. These calls are profiled based on language and on what cell tower they bounce off of. If dispatch suspects that the caller is crossing the border, then the call is routed to a special Border Patrol line—which nobody ever picks up. I'm not exaggerating. If you doubt me, gentle reader, I encourage you to go stand in the middle of the desert, call 911, explain in Spanish that you are lost and in need of help, and see for yourself what happens. For what it's worth, this is completely illegal under a whole raft of American laws—it's as if dispatch would never send an ambulance in response to calls from the inner city in which the caller "sounds black." (Oh, wait a minute…). Still, it happens every day.

On some occasions, travelers in distress have called 911, been told that there is not enough information to initiate a search, then called their families, who then called their consulates, who then called *us. We* then went and found the caller standing at some known point, exactly where they said they were. There are actually only a finite number of places with "two cattle tanks, one empty and one full, next to three windmills, southeast of a mountain that looks like an elephant and southwest of one that looks like a camel," and so on. This has happened more than once, despite the fact that the government is capable of using geo-location to triangulate cell phones and we are not—along with other obvious differences in the scale of resources available to our network and that of the state.

"If you hear the dogs, keep going. If you see the torches in the woods, keep going. If there's shouting after you, keep going. Don't ever stop. Keep going. If you want a taste of freedom, keep going."

– Attributed to Harriet Tubman, although possibly apocryphal.

Hillary Clinton used this quote as a metaphor in her speech at the 2008 Democratic National Convention, and continued to do so during her 2016 presidential campaign—while the administration that she worked for had been hunting people with dogs every single day for eight years. I take the message more literally.

Designed to Kill

Who Benefits?

The suffering that takes place every day on the border is not an accident. It is not a mistake and it is not the result of a misunderstanding. It is the predictable and intentional result of policies implemented at every level of government on both sides of the border. These policies have rational objectives and directly benefit identifiable sectors of the population of both countries. It may be evil, but it's not stupid. If this sounds a little shrill, let me explain how I've seen this play out on the ground.

When I started working in the desert, I began to notice some very peculiar things about the Border Patrol's operations. They would do a lot of enforcement in some areas and very little in others, and this would not necessarily correspond to which areas were busy and which areas were slow. In fact, often the enforcement would take place in such a way that it would push traffic *into* rather than out of the busiest areas, where Border Patrol would keep a low profile until the very northern end of the route. At that point, there would be a moderate amount of enforcement again, but not really what you would expect given the numbers of people that were moving through.

Then they started building lots of surveillance towers. But once again, the towers were not really built in the places where the traffic was heaviest—they were built on the edges of them. If anything, they seemed to be intent on forcing traffic into the busiest routes rather than out of them. What was happening? Meanwhile, I was constantly meeting migrants whose groups had been split up by helicopters. The Border Patrol would fly over them a few feet off the ground, everybody would run in different directions, and soon there would be thirty people wandering lost across the desert in groups of two or three. What seemed particularly odd was that the Border Patrol often made no effort to actually apprehend these groups after breaking them up—they just flew away. Why?

> "Answer the question of who benefits or profits most directly from an action, event, or outcome and you always have the starting point for your analysis or investigation, and sometimes it will also give you the end point."

> – *Sir Arthur Conan Doyle*

We got a call from the Mexican consulate. A man's family had contacted them. He had been missing for nine days. The last time anybody had seen him, he was somewhere near a small body of water with a fractured rib. They thought that he was in our area somewhere. We searched and searched for about a week, but we never found him. His brother, who had papers, came up with a horse. He combed the desert on horseback for another week and eventually found his brother's body.

Two weeks later, a man came walking into camp. He was carrying an almost empty gallon jug of water with our markings on it in one hand, and a white shirt tied to a long stick in the other. He stuck the jug under my nose: "This water saved my life! I was praying to Jesus for water! I was sure I was going to die, and I found this water in the desert! I think Border Patrol leaves it on the trails for people!"

"No, man," I said, "Border Patrol couldn't give a shit if people live or die. We left that water."

"Those bastards," he said. "I've been waving this flag at their helicopters for three days. They just fly on. When you want them they're nowhere to be seen, and when you don't—there they are." I checked the markings on the bottle. It had been dropped two weeks earlier, at an unusual location we had only gone to because we were looking for the man who died.

And then there's this. Over the years, No More Deaths has developed a pretty comprehensive understanding of the area we cover, which at times has been one of the most heavily traveled sections of the entire border. We've formed a fairly clear picture of where traffic starts, where it goes, how it gets there, where it's busy and where it's slow at any given time, where the pinch points are, and so on. I honestly believe that if I worked for the Border Patrol, I could basically point at a map and tell them how to shut down the whole sector. It's really not rocket science. Keep in mind that all of our work has been done by untrained civilian volunteers, armed with low-end GPS units, a few old trucks, run-of-the-mill mapping software, cheap cell phones with spotty service, and a very limited budget. Does it seem logical that we could figure this stuff out while the government of the United States of America cannot, despite access to helicopters, unmanned drones, electronic sensors, fleets of well-maintained trucks, night vision systems, state-of-the-art communications and surveillance and mapping technology, tens of thousands of paid employees, and a limitless supply of money to shovel down the hole at every possible opportunity?

I don't think it does. So what's going on?

If you accept the stated objectives of the border at face value, then none of this makes any sense at all. If you accept that the actual objectives may not be the stated ones, things start to come together fast. The task of the Border Patrol—and the actual objective of the policies it is there to enforce—is *not* to stop illegal immigration. It is to manage and control that migration.

But to what end? To whose benefit? Settle in, because it's complicated.

First of all, it's as plain as day that the American economy is dependent in no small part on the exploitation of undocumented labor. You know it's true, I know it's true, the Guatemalans installing the air conditioning at the Trump International Hotel know it's true, but it is considered extremely taboo to mention this fact in public. Excuse me, but anyone with a modicum of common sense should be able to see that if the government actually builds a two-thousand-mile-long Berlin Wall and then rounds up and deports every one of the nearly twelve million undocumented people in the country, there will be massive and immediate disruption in the agriculture and animal exploitation industries, not to mention in everything related to construction—quite possibly leading to a serious breakdown in the national food distribution network and conceivably even famine. I'm not exaggerating.

The people who write border policies are not fools. They understand this perfectly, even if most of the people who voted Donald Trump into office do not. Regardless of what any politician says, I seriously doubt that anyone is going to put a stop to illegal immigration as long as undocumented labor is needed to maintain the stability of the economic system. I'll believe it when I see it. But this isn't good news to those of us who dislike seeing people treated abysmally, because what's more important is that this migration will continue to be managed and controlled.

The border is a sick farce with a deadly conclusion. The goal is to make entering the country without papers extremely dangerous, traumatizing, and expensive—but *possible*. The point isn't to deter people from coming—far from it. It is to ensure that when they do come, the threat of deportation will mean something very serious. It means spending a ton of money. It means risking your life to return. It means that you may never see your family again. This is supposed to provide American employers with a vast and disposable pool of labor that is vulnerable and therefore easy to exploit—and this in turn drives down wages for workers with American citizenship, which is why the old saw about the "illegals coming to our country and taking our jobs" is so convincing. Like many good lies, it's powerful because it omits the most important part of the truth.*

Those who believe that immigration and border enforcement protect the jobs or wages of American workers are seriously misinterpreting the situation. Even if you limit the scope of your analysis to market-based behavior, it seems clear that if undocumented workers were not subjected to such extraordinary risks and pressures they would act like anybody else and obtain the highest price for their labor that the market would bear. In fact, these same workers have proven themselves able time and again to struggle successfully for higher wages, despite having to overcome obstacles other workers do not face. But border and immigration enforcement drives down wages across the board—that's *the point of it.*

Here's another lead that is easy to follow:

Immigrants from Mexico and Central America serve as the stand-in bogeyman of American politics, always there to pop out of the closet if nothing scarier is at hand.† Anti-immigrant fearmongering waxes and wanes precisely with the apparent threat of jihadi terrorism. Whenever a clear and present danger

---

* The lie becomes even more believable when self-described liberals—to be precise, neoliberals—respond with a falsehood of their own: "They're doing the jobs that American workers don't want to do." Wrong. The United States contains millions of chronically unemployed and underemployed unskilled and semi-skilled workers with American citizenship. Many of them would be quite happy to perform many of the jobs now done by undocumented workers, if those jobs paid their actual value on the open market (say $15 an hour) instead of the artificially low wages (say $6-8 dollars an hour) that are only possible because of immigration enforcement and unequal exchange. I should know; I'm one of those workers.

† America has rotated a variety of identities through this position over the years. See "Heteropatriachy and the Three Pillars of White Supremacy" by Andrea Smith, which defines the "savage," the "brute," and the "foreigner" as the core national tropes, called upon to justify genocide, slavery, and war respectively. This is a useful text, but I feel that I should mention that the author got herself into a world of trouble by publicly claiming for years to be Cherokee when in fact she is not.

is lacking, the so-called immigration debate becomes the de facto national security issue for politicians.

There are two other factors complicating this equation: the state of the American economy and the state of American social movements. Anti-immigrant sentiment becomes more prominent when the economy is weak and needs less undocumented labor; it becomes less prominent when the economy is strong and needs more.* Likewise, it waxes when social movements are weak and wanes when they are strong.† This is the algebra of American anxiety: fill in the values and you can do the math. Both of the American political parties are always seeking to capitalize on these dynamics as best they can.

The Democratic strategy is nuanced. First, they blame Republicans for the lack of progress on immigration issues. They hope that this will maintain the support of voters from immigrant communities. Second, they do not actually push any pro-immigrant measures unless they experience severe pressure from their base to do so; if the Obama administration did anything worthwhile in the sphere of immigration reform, such pressure is the sole reason why. The Democrats hope that this inaction will appease anti-immigrant voters. Third, they ramped up the rate of deportations to levels never before seen or even imagined. Every single year, the Obama administration deported more people than any previous administration ever did in one year—something like 400,000 annually. Deportations rose steadily from 2009 to 2013, dropped somewhat in 2014 and 2015, and spiked again in 2016 as the administration attempted to deport those who crossed during the 2013-2014 period discussed above. All this assumes that the notoriously elastic state statistics can be trusted, which is not a safe bet.

* Border enforcement does the same thing.
† One of the unrecognized accomplishments of the Occupy movement was that it shifted the ground of the immigration debate. The scapegoating of immigrants was most intense from the beginning of the financial collapse in 2008 to the onset of Occupy in fall 2011. Then, suddenly, it became acceptable to blame things on bankers and the financial sector rather than on undocumented people. This helped compel the Obama administration to make the policy changes of 2013-2014.

The Democrats can use those numbers to tout their law-and-order credentials when they need to court conservative voters. Conversely, they can produce other numbers to make themselves look compassionate when it is more expedient to pander to liberals. The party played out this "Peanuts" routine for eight solid years, except that in this version Charlie Brown not only misses the football but also gets thrown under the bus. The case could be made that the Republicans would have been better, since they would have been less nervous about being outflanked to the right on national security. This strategy worked out nicely for the Democrats, if less so for the hundreds of thousands of families they tore apart or for the thousands of people whose bones are strewn across the desert. As I write this, they are shuffling off the stage, every promise broken, meekly handing the reins of power to white nationalists. Thanks and good night, everybody: we couldn't have done it without you.

The Republican strategy is more straightforward: they appeal directly to fear and racism. Evidently, this is still a winning ticket.[‡] Nevertheless, one can win a battle and still lose a war. Donald Trump's election notwithstanding, the party's stupidity is breathtaking. Had they been in their right minds, the Republicans would have passed some kind of immigration reform and amnesty act during the first Bush administration, as the Reagan administration did in 1986. They could have gotten away with anything after the September 11 attacks; we all know what they got away with instead. Had they passed such a reform, they would have sewn up the Latino vote for a generation, and their party would have been able to retain power for the foreseeable future.

‡ Roughly a million more people voted Republican in 2016 than in 2012; roughly a million more did so in 2012 than in 2008. Roughly six million fewer people voted Democratic in 2016 as in 2008, and Clinton still won the popular vote. So, the lesson of the 2016 elections is not that the Republican base is suddenly drastically larger, especially considering that the population has increased by nearly 20 million since 2008. Rather, it is that after eight years of disappointment, a sizable percentage of the Democratic base appears to have lost faith in the political process.

Instead, they ignored the country's changing demographics and doubled down on white supremacy.

This gambit paid off at least one more time, and the Republicans have irrevocably defined themselves as the party of crude xenophobia and retrograde white power—to an increasingly multi-racial country and a generation raised on hip-hop. In the long run, I don't believe that is a winning strategy. Most likely, it will come back to haunt them, in 2020 if not sooner. When it does, it may well tear the party apart, if not the country.

Here's one last clue to understanding the real purpose of the border: much of the legislation that becomes government policy is written by the corporations that stand to profit from it. Arizona's State Bill 1070, which was intended to require police to lock up anyone they stop who cannot show proof of having entered the country legally, was drafted in December 2009 at the Grand Hyatt hotel in Washington D.C. by officials of the billion-dollar Corrections Corporation of America (CCA), the largest private prison company in the country.* This took place at a meeting of the American Legislative Exchange Council (ALEC), a membership organization of state legislators and powerful corporations. The law, which was partially overturned but provided the model for copycat legislation that passed in other states, was designed to send hundreds of thousands of immigrants to prison—which means hundreds of millions of dollars in profits for the companies such as CCA that are responsible for housing them. It is not in this industry's interest to completely stop illegal immigration; it is in their interest to let in enough people to fill their jails.

So who benefits from the death in the desert? In a broad sense, the entire ruling class does. But that's not the whole story, not by any means. To tell that story, we have to back up a bit.

To recap, the passage of NAFTA in 1994 decimated the Mexican agricultural sector and set off a tsunami of migration to the United States. Within the year, the Clinton administration launched Operation Gatekeeper, a program that massively increased

* CCA changed their name to CoreCivic after they lost the contract to run prisons through the Bureau of Prisons.

funding for Border Patrol operations in the San Diego sector of the border in California. The federal government greatly stepped up enforcement in this sector and built a fourteen-mile wall between San Diego and Tijuana. Operation Gatekeeper marked the beginning of a two-decade-running process of ever-increasing border militarization that continued steadily throughout the Clinton, Bush, and Obama administrations, and will undoubtedly continue to do so during the Trump administration. Every year, there have been more Border Patrol agents, National Guardsmen, helicopters, fences, towers, checkpoints, sensors, guns, and dogs along the border.

By all accounts I've ever heard, it used to be much easier to cross the border than it is now.[†] Most people crossed into relatively safer urbanized areas such as San Diego, El Paso, or the Lower Rio Grande Valley in Texas. Starting with Operation Gatekeeper, the Border Patrol made it much more difficult to enter the country in these places; over the years, it has methodically pushed traffic into the increasingly remote mountains and deserts beyond, contributing to the death toll. At this point, I think, the game is reaching an endpoint. The government has pushed the traffic into the very deepest and deadliest pockets of the entire border, which is where they want it. This does not mean that the situation is completely static—the Border Patrol will clamp down on some of these pockets sometimes and ease up on others—but on the large scale, it has been more or less stable for many years. It remains to be seen if the new administration will fundamentally change this.

These changes have produced several interesting side effects. As I said, in decades past, many people used to come to the US to work for a season, then return home until the next year. That's much less common now that getting into the country is such an ordeal. People come and generally stay as long as they can.

Also, most people who crossed used to be men with families south of the border. There are many more women and children crossing now that it's no longer feasible for most men to work in

† In our sector, it was definitely easier in 2008 than in 2016.

the north without leaving their families behind for good. Finally, with the increase in internal deportations, there are many more people crossing now who have lived here for long periods of time and are returning to their homes in the United States. This latter group faces a particularly fiendish dilemma if they run into trouble on the way. I have often heard people whose children live south of the border say things like "I thought I was going to die and all I could think about was my babies. It's better for me to go back home than to risk dying again." I have often heard people whose children live north of the border say things like "If I have to risk dying to get home to my babies, then I will."

My colleague and I were driving down the road. There were three men standing there—a young guy, an old guy, and a really big guy. "How are you doing?" I asked them.

"Not very good," said the young guy. "Our guide left us and we've been totally lost for days. We're exhausted and we can't go on any more. Can you just call the Border Patrol to come and pick us up?"

"Yeah, I can do that if you're sure that's what you want," I told him. "They drive this road all the time. I'm kind of surprised they haven't seen you yet."

"Yes, please call them. We don't want to do this anymore."

"You're sure?"

"Yes."

I called the Border Patrol and gave them our position. While we were waiting, the young guy and the old guy sat close to each other, and the big guy lay down on the other side of the road with his arms behind his head and his feet propped up on a rock. It was clear that the young guy and the old guy were good friends, and that neither of them liked the big guy very much. They called him *Flaco*, meaning "Skinny," which was not very nice, since he decidedly was not. "That guy is an absolute bastard," said the young guy. "I hope I never see him again in my life."

A while later, he asked my colleague if he could use his phone. "My wife and baby daughter live in Los Angeles," he said. "I want to tell them that I'm OK." He took the phone and went off to make the call.

Ten minutes later he came back. Before leaving he had been calm and collected. Now he looked utterly distraught and had tears running down his face. "Fuck this!" he said. "I'm leaving. My baby is sick. She needs me. Where am I? How do I get out of here? Which way is north? Do you have any water I can take? Do you have any quarters?"

"Jesus!" I said. "I called the Border Patrol like an hour ago. They're going to be here any minute. What do you want to do?"

"I'm getting out of here," he said.

The old guy came running up to him. "What's going on?" he asked. "Are you OK?"

"Carina is sick. She needs me. I'm going to see her."

"Wait, that's crazy," said the old guy. "How are you—"

"How far is it? Do you have any food?" the young guy asked me.

"I think it's a really bad idea for you to go by yourself," I told him. "You might die, and that wouldn't do your daughter any good. Maybe you should go back, rest, get with another group, and try again in a week or two."

He shook his head, still crying. "She might need an operation. It's going to be really expensive. I can't afford to pay to cross again. I don't have time to talk. They're coming. *Ya vienen.*" He started to walk toward the mountains.

The old guy looked at me, looked at him, looked at me again, and looked back at him. "Wait, Paco, OK, I'll go with you."

I stuffed as much food and water into their hands as I could. "Do you see those mountains way over there? Go that way. When you get close, go towards those other ones. The freeway is over there. If you need help, that's the only place you're going to find it. Do you have any money?" They both shook their heads. I gave them five dollars. It is the gospel truth that at that point in time it was the last five dollars I had to my name. They left.

Flaco had not stirred this whole time. "I don't like this one bit," my colleague told me. "You just called BP on three guys and they're going to get here and find one? That's not good."

"Yeah," I said. "Let's get out of here." I went to Flaco. "Um, we're gonna go," I told him. "Here's some more food and water. They always take a long time to come but they will get here. Just don't go anywhere, OK?"

"Sure, whatever," he said. We drove away, and I never found out what happened to any of them.

As I hope I have made clear, a policy of pushing migrant traffic into extremely dangerous areas does not imply an actual intention to stop or even deter people from entering the country illegally. This complex and perverse strategy has numerous advantages. It allows politicians to look tough for the cameras while still providing the American economy with the farmworkers and meatpackers it depends on. It provides ample opportunities to swing huge government contracts to giant corporations—for example, to Wackenhut and G4S to transport migrants, to Corrections Corporation of America to detain them, to Boeing to build surveillance infrastructure. It justifies the hefty salaries of the 20,000 people who work for the Border Patrol. And it has other beneficiaries, whom I will speak of shortly. On the whole, border militarization is best understood as a massive government pork and corporate welfare project that is probably only surpassed in the last twenty years by the war in Iraq.

The outcome of this policy has been most educational. Just as it used to be easier to cross the border, it also used to be a lot cheaper. This won't be surprising to anyone familiar with the laws of supply and demand. Any service will become more expensive if it becomes more difficult to provide, and the service of being smuggled across the border has certainly been a case study in this law. Prices rose and rose as the Border Patrol pushed people further and further from the cities and established more and more checkpoints that made the journey longer and longer, until at a certain point there was as much money to be made in moving people as there was in moving drugs. At that point, the cartels that already controlled the drug trade recognized an excellent business opportunity, muscled out the competition, and took over the game.

This transformed what had been a relatively low-key affair into a lucrative, highly centralized, and increasingly brutal industry with tens of billions of dollars at stake. There is no doubt that these cartels are among the primary beneficiaries of American and Mexican drug, trade, and immigration policies since the end of the Cold War.

Unsurprisingly, the rise of the cartels to a position of absolute dominance within a booming industry led to a mass-based approach and an extraordinarily inhumane methodology. I have commonly heard the organizations referred to as *pollero* networks, which means something like "meat herders," since *pollo* is the word for a dead chicken rather than a live one. This should offer some indication of the degree of care that these organizations tend to invest in each individual human life throughout the process of bringing people into the United States. I have seen groups of as many as fifty people—and heard about groups as large as a hundred—being driven quite literally like cattle across the desert, with the sick and wounded straggling behind and trying desperately to keep up. I have met people who were told that what is always at best an extremely demanding four- to five-day journey would take as little as twelve hours on foot, and countless more who were left behind to die by their guides without hesitation when they were no longer able to keep up.

As a result of border militarization, prices have risen now to the point that it can cost over ten thousand dollars for Central Americans to be brought into the United States through the networks. Fees for Mexicans vary widely, but they are far from cheap.

You won't be surprised to hear that many people who wish to migrate do not actually have ten thousand dollars lying around. The cartels have developed a variety of inventive solutions to this problem, often involving kidnapping and indentured servitude. I've met people who spent years working in the United States simply to pay off their initial fee, some while held in conditions of outright bonded labor. I've met others who made it through the desert and were immediately held for ransom by the same groups that brought them in. The ones who were able to raise a few thousand dollars more were allowed to go. The ones who

weren't able to were beaten for days and then driven back out to be left in the desert, where Border Patrol agents who clearly had some sort of working arrangement with the kidnappers picked them up for deportation within minutes. I'm not kidding. It's scandalous.

Like the Three Kings, Nacho, Chucho, and Don Bigotes showed up just before Christmas. They had been together through thick and thin.

Chucho was from Mexico City and in his early twenties. He was big, strong, and laconic. You could tell that he knew how to handle his business in a fistfight. Chucho was a talented graffiti writer, made excellent beats, and could quote lyrics by rappers from Madrid to Santiago. Basically, he was a b-boy, and he would have fit in anywhere around the world where hip-hop sub-culture is recognized. He had an active social media presence, to say the least.

Nacho was in his late thirties and Honduran. He had lived and worked without papers in Mexico for over 15 years. To pull this off, he had developed an amazing ability to code-switch between Mexican and Honduran Spanish. When he wanted, he could sound like a quintessential Honduran. As needed, he could turn on a dime, recalibrate much of his vocabulary, all of his slang, as well as a fair amount of his grammar, and sound exactly like a Mexican. To this day, I've never met anyone who was quite so good at this. Additionally, Nacho was an astoundingly industrious person. He simply could not sit still. He would cook everybody breakfast, do all the dishes, clean up the kitchen, sweep out the medical tent, organize all the clothes and backpacks and shoes, check the oil in the trucks, sort the recycling, take out the trash, fill buckets of compost for the toilets and bags of water for the showers, and crawl under the trailer to chase away raccoons with a broom; all before noon. He would do more in an hour than a normal volunteer does in a day. We should have paid him to stay at camp. He also liked to hug people. He would give me a good morning hug, a hug when I left camp, a hug when I returned, a hug for dinner, and a hug goodnight. It never got old. Nacho was truly a good-hearted human being. He was also very short.

As memorable as both Nacho and Chucho were, however, Don Bigotes was the real prize. He was fifty-four and tougher than a boot. Born in Jalisco, he had lived for thirty-five years in the United States, working all over the country as a pipefitter, heavy equipment operator, hard rock miner, oil field rough-neck, and at all sorts of other hard labor. He wore a mustache so huge, so fierce, and so virile that it could only be referred to in the honorific and the plural. *Everybody* called him Don Bigotes.* Not only did he look like Pancho Villa's older brother, he talked like him, too—in a rumbling baritone growl punctu-ated by jaw-dropping curses and memorable turns of phrase. The first time I saw him with his shirt off I noticed that he had a bullet wound through his lower back, with a matching exit wound in front.

"Some fucking guy shot me in a laundromat in Wyoming," he said. "In 1987." And that was that.

This trio had been through hell together, and had been around each other twenty-four hours a day for weeks on end. The dynamics of their partnership were hilarious. One time, Chucho and I were talking about Don Bigotes and what an epic character he was.

"Has he told you about when that guy whose wife he was sleeping with shot him in the laundromat yet?" Chucho asked me, his eyes gleaming mischievously. He cackled triumphantly when I told him that Don Bigotes had omitted this salacious detail.

The most priceless interactions, however, were between Nacho and Don Bigotes. Occasionally, Don Bigotes would descend into a truly foul mood. I didn't blame him. The country that he called home had disowned and rejected him after accepting thirty-five years of his labor, leaving him stranded in the desert on Christmas a thousand miles away from his family after narrowly escaping death. His anger at the whole situation was terrifying to behold. At times like these, the two men had a ritual.

* Mr. Mustaches or, better yet, *Sir Mustaches.*

"Don Bigotes!" Nacho would exclaim. "You are not well! You are upset! You need a hug!"

"No, I do not," Don Bigotes would respond, staring straight ahead with his fists clenched at his side, looking like he wanted to murder God. "Do not hug me, Nacho."

"Yes! Yes, I will! I will hug you, Don Bigotes!"

"Do not hug me, Nacho. I do not want you to hug me."

"I am! I'm hugging you now, Don Bigotes!"

"Stop hugging me, Nacho."

"I will not! I will not stop hugging you, Don Bigotes!"

And so on.

Some weeks after this trio left camp, I finally heard what happened to them afterwards. In the desert, Nacho and Don Bigotes were separated from Chucho. They made it to Phoenix together. Chucho made it out of the desert on his own, several days later. When the truck arrived to pick him up, he did a very smart thing. He texted the number of the license plate to Don Bigotes. When the truck arrived at the safehouse, he did another very smart thing. He texted the address to Don Bigotes, along with the name and phone number of his point of contact. Chucho was no fool.

So, when the traffickers took his phone from him and told him that they would beat him and dump him in the desert if his family didn't come up with another $3000 within twenty-four hours, Chucho stayed calm. He knew what would happen next. When Chucho stopped answering his phone, Don Bigotes called the number that Chucho had sent him, and this is what he said, in his rumbling baritone growl, sounding exactly like the scariest man on earth:

"Listen to me, Julio, you piece of shit. You are confused. You do not seem to understand. You do not know me, but I know you. You live in a brown adobe house with black shutters and a blue door, across the street from a *taqueria.* You drive a gray 2006 Chevy Silverado with a lift kit and a dent in the rear left quarter panel. In my hand I hold a phone, Julio, you misbegotten son of a mangy flea-bitten bitch. Who will I call with this phone? Will I call the migra? Will I call the police? Perhaps I will think of someone else to call. Perhaps I will call someone to drive by your house, to see what your wife looks like or where your children go to school. Perhaps I will find you myself, and perhaps with my own hands I will hang you by your fucking neck until you are dead. *You* will not tell *me* what *I* will do, Julio, *I* will tell *you* what *you* will do. You will let my friend Chucho go free, or else I will have *options.*"

They let Chucho walk right out the door, and twenty minutes later Don Bigotes picked him up at a gas station in south Phoenix. The last I heard, Nacho and Don Bigotes were planting trees together in Texas.

As bad as all this is, it still doesn't fully convey the depth of the cruelty that has characterized this era of government-sponsored cartel control. Rape and sexual assault of female migrants is absolutely endemic at every step of the process—as it is to varying degrees for transgender migrants and younger or smaller men. This has been greatly exacerbated by the policies of the US government: by pushing the traffic out into the middle of nowhere, they have basically guaranteed that in order to enter the country women and children have to place themselves in situations in which rape and sexual assault are extremely likely.

In addition, the trails are frequented by groups of armed bandits who make their living targeting migrants. I believe that some of the bandits are employed by the cartels themselves, who are simply robbing their own clients, while others are freelancers taking advantage of an easy opportunity to prey on defenseless people who are often carrying their life savings in their pockets. Again, it is primarily because the US government has pushed the traffic to the ends of the earth that these fuckers have been blessed with such favorable circumstances in which to ply their trade.*

* Banditry targeting migrants was particularly widespread on the American side of the Arivaca sector until about 2010, when somebody (probably up the Sinaloa food chain) put a stop to it. Around this time, a friend of ours found the bodies of three men not far from one of our water drops, hung by nooses around their necks, swinging from a tree, with notes pinned to

To be fair, I've also heard stories of low-level cartel members acting decently and compassionately, even heroically. It's worth pointing out that the *guias* (guides)—the people who actually walk the groups through the desert to the other side of the checkpoints—are at the very bottom of the pecking order within the networks.[†] Their lives are considered nearly as expendable as those of the migrants. Working in the desert has given me some appreciation for the fact that being a guide would be very stressful. They're supposed to bring large groups of people through harsh terrain where there is no potable water, usually in the dark or in brutal heat, while being hunted by military personnel with guns and helicopters. Their bosses are probably not the kind of people you want to run afoul of. It's hardly surprising that guides are often unwilling to risk losing their whole group because one or two people can't keep up. The whole situation is guaranteed to bring out the worst in someone.

This is not to make excuses for them, or to absolve relatively powerless people of their personal responsibility when they do indefensible things. It is simply to say that most of the guilt has to be assigned to the powerful people whose actions have created this nightmare and who profit most directly from it.

There are good guides. Some of them are incredibly skilled. We've heard many stories of guides who did everything in their power to take care of the people in their group, and stories of guides who took in stragglers at no financial gain to themselves.

The ultimate story of this kind took place in 2005. A group of our volunteers ran into a group of migrants in the desert. One of them was carrying a *baby deer* on his back. "Thank god!" he

their chests reading *"This is what we do to thieves."* I wasn't surprised; it had gotten that bad. Banditry is less frequent there now, although I've no doubt it remains common along other parts of the border.

† In the northwest, the *guias* tend to come from the same demographic as the marijuana smugglers: haggard young men from northern Sonora. I've no doubt that they have counterparts in the northeast.

said. "We found this little guy tied to a tree. Some hunter must have been using him as bait for mountain lions. We couldn't just leave him there; it wouldn't have been right. We've been carrying him with us for days. But he's really heavy, and we don't know what we're going to do with him when we get picked up. They're not going to let us put him in the van. Can you please take him and find him a home?"

I've personally run into two different migrant groups who were accompanied by stray dogs, both of whom made this same request. The deer and both dogs were driven out of the desert to safety. The irony is that it's legal to drive a dog or a deer out of danger—but if you do it for a person, you go to prison.

There are also really bad guides. We've heard many stories of abuse. "Everybody talks about us like we're the fucking devil," a burro told me once. "Some of these fucking *guias* are the real devils. At least we all know what we're getting into. These guys, they beat people and abuse women and leave kids in the middle of fucking nowhere if they can't keep up. Some of those dudes are just total fucking shitbags." It is easy to demonize drug smugglers, but the behavior of some guides is simply beyond the pale.

There are also a lot of guides who are capable of acting either decently or indecently, cruelly or compassionately, heroically or atrociously, depending on the pressures they are under and how they respond to them. The guides themselves are used and discarded by their employers as quickly as tires.

Toward that end, permit me to say another word on the relationship between the governments and the cartels. Basically it is this: they need each other. They are animated by the same logic and they share similar interests.

Perhaps it is most precise to make a distinction between the situations in the US and in Mexico. In the United States, the cartels need the government, while the government makes great use of the cartels. The cartels rely on the US government to keep the prices of their goods and services artificially high, while the government uses the cartels to justify funneling billions of dollars to the transnational corporations whose interests they represent. On the Mexican side, as I argued above, it isn't realistic to talk about the government and the cartels as if they are separate entities. There, the government and the various cartels are fighting for control of the multi-billion dollar American drug and migration market.

Analysts sometime use the term "Colombianization" to point out that the state of affairs in Mexico is starting to look a lot like that in Colombia. Perhaps the most striking similarity is in the increasingly sophisticated collusion between elements of the government and the cartels with which they are nominally at war.

On a local and state level, it is extremely common for all of the cartels to buy off police, mayors, judges, and other government officials. On the national level, strong evidence suggests that the Mexican Army and federal government are favoring the Sinaloa Cartel—the largest and richest in the nation—in hopes that it will eventually defeat its rivals and work out a stable agreement with the government such as the one enjoyed by their counterparts in Colombia.

There is indeed a great deal of cartel infiltration of the Mexican security forces. This is common on the American side as well, though less widespread. In general, however, the arrangement on both sides of the border is not so crude that there always or even usually has to be direct personnel overlap between, say, the Corrections Corporation of America, the Border Patrol, the Gulf Cartel, and the Mexican Army. What's most important is that all of these organizations have interlocking interests, benefit from each other's activities, and generally act in a way that keeps each other in business. This unholy trinity of government, corporations, and organized crime—three ways of saying the same thing—is a formidable opponent to anyone who hopes to see the death in the desert end any time soon.

The Border Patrol

Allow me a couple of words about the Border Patrol. There is no government job that can be attained without a high school diploma that pays more than that of a Border Patrol agent. They are generally paid about $45,000 for their first year, $55,000 the next two, and $70,000 and up after that. They are not going around hungry.

I don't know how to convey the extent of the abuse that I have heard migrants report at the hands of these agents.[*] I have heard of agents beating, sexually abusing, and shooting people as well as throwing them into cactus, stealing their money, denying detainees food and water, deporting unaccompanied minors, and driving around wildly with migrants chained in the back of trucks that look unmistakably like animal control vehicles—not to mention robbing smugglers and otherwise demonstrating extensive involvement in drug trafficking.

We were deep in the mountains near the border. There were seven of us. It was late afternoon and we had been walking all day. We were in a deep wash, approaching a very heavily used migrant trail, when someone shouted from the hill up above us. "HEY! *HEY!*" Three people came running down the hill at full speed, cutting through catclaw and cactus, and jumped into the wash. There was an older man, a younger man, and a teenage girl whose legs were covered with half dried scabs and bleeding cuts. The older man pulled a bible out of his pocket and threw it down open on a large rock in front of me. "PHILIPPIANS FOUR THIRTEEN!" he declared, in English, pointing. "I CAN DO ANYTHING THROUGH THE POWER OF CHRIST WHICH STRENGTHENS ME!"

"What?"

[*] See the No More Deaths abuse documentation reports *Crossing the Line* (2008), *A Culture of Cruelty* (2011), *Post-deportation Health* (2012), and *Shakedown* (2014) for extensive source material.

All three spoke at once: "There were big dogs!" "They were biting people!" "They were pulling them down and biting them!" "They were screaming and they were biting them!"

"What? Wait! What?" I said.

"There were about thirty of us," the girl explained in perfect English. "The migra were waiting for us at the pass up there. They had dogs. They turned the dogs on us. The dogs were biting people, and pulling them down, and biting them on the ground. People were screaming and bleeding and running in every direction. We ran down the mountain. They shouted at us to stop but we kept running. I don't know if anyone else got away."

"This was how long ago?" I asked her.

"Ten minutes."

"Ten minutes!"

"Yeah, ten or fifteen." The men nodded.

"We have to get the fuck out of here."

"Yes," she agreed.

The ten of us ran through the mountains. The older man occasionally broke out into song—sometimes Madonna, sometimes Beyoncé, usually Shakira. "I'm on tonight! You know my hips don't lie!" He would pause periodically to demonstrate the veracity of this statement. "You know—Shakira! It helps to sing!" We passed a shrine where other migrants had left candles and bracelets and rosaries and offerings to the Virgin of Guadalupe. The younger man knelt, crossed himself, and said a prayer, nearly without breaking stride. After about two hours, we stopped in a side canyon and dressed some of the girl's wounds.

"How old are you?" I asked her.

"Fifteen. I've lived in Oregon since I was two. I got into trouble. What am I going to do in Mexico? I've never lived there. I don't have any people there. I haven't been able to talk to my mom since I got deported. I'm just going to have to keep trying this until I make it."

"She's very strong," said the younger man.

"As for me," the older man said, "it doesn't really matter. When I'm in Mexico I live on the street. I come here and I live on the street. It's all the same."

"He's a nice guy," said the girl. "There was a woman who was having a hard time keeping up. He carried her bag for her, and told us jokes and sang us songs."

We stopped again at dark. They ate and ate, and the older man told stories. "We're going to keep going," the younger man said at last. "We're going to get some sleep and leave when the moon comes up."

"It's a very long way, and it's easy to get lost," I told him. "Do you know how to get there?"

"I know exactly how to get there," he said. We talked about the mountains and I could tell that he was telling the truth.

"Do you want to call your mom?" I asked the girl.

"No, she'll just worry. I'll call her when I make it."

I don't know what happened to them. A few days later, there was a small article in the Nogales paper about a large group of migrants who were deported with wounds from dog bites and needed treatment on the Mexican side.

Border Patrol is a lucrative business in and of itself, and part of that business entails exaggerating the danger of the job in order to milk taxpayers for more money. In my experience, law enforcement personnel in general consider their work to be truly perilous, believing that the world owes them a debt of gratitude and a fat paycheck. Since inception of the institution in 1904, 122 Border Patrol agents have died in action, 40 of whom were victims of homicide. In 2015, out of some 20,000 agents, not one of them lost his or her life in the line of duty. It is impossible to know how many migrants die crossing the border every year, but somewhere between the middle hundreds and the low thousands is probably a good bet. If you crunch the numbers, you will find that Border Patrol agents are also much safer than roofers, sanitation workers, truck drivers, sex workers, and any number of other people whose jobs are actually dangerous.

The other thing that any self-respecting Border Patrol agent will tell you is that they are protecting us from terrorists. This begs the question of who "us" is. More human beings have lost their lives in the desert as a direct result of Border Patrol activity than in every ISIS and Al-Qaeda attack on American soil combined—and quite possibly more than would have died even if every attack that the Border Patrol has had a hand in thwarting or deterring had been successful. The more important point is that as long as there is such outrageous global inequality, Americans are never really going to be safe.

Many Border Patrol agents come from working class backgrounds; many are Latino. To be fair, I acknowledge that I have met some who treated migrants with respect. I also allow that in fact they do find people in distress sometimes, that some of those people would surely have died otherwise, and that some agents can be nice enough. The fact of the matter, though, is that it is rank-and-file Border Patrol agents who enforce the policies that cause all of the problems I am describing. No matter what they do individually, they will never be a part of the solution as long as they wear a uniform, carry a gun, and obey orders. They could put the cartels out of business and end the death in the desert tomorrow simply by going home.

I've heard too many apologies for the Border Patrol—they are not the enemy, they are subject to the same economic forces as the migrants, and so on. I don't buy it. History is replete with examples of people who were willing to sell out their own people to save themselves. There were Black slave drivers on the plantations, Jewish police in the ghetto, Native scouts leading the army after Crazy Horse, and now there are Latino Border Patrol agents in the desert. Sorry, but I'm not impressed. I think that when people become willing accomplices in atrocities, they just don't deserve much sympathy.

Recently, a friend of mine found the body of a woman who died of some combination of dehydration, sickness, exposure, and exhaustion within a quarter of a mile of one of our largest supply drops—a place that I have personally serviced several hundred times. She had passed through an area where for months, a few particularly hostile Border Patrol agents consistently slashed our water bottles, popped the tops off cans of beans so that they would go rancid, and removed the blankets that we

> "Nobody in the world, nobody in history, has ever gotten their freedom by appealing to the moral sense of the people who were oppressing them."

> – Assata Shakur

leave on the trails. As a result of these activities, we have had to move these drops around constantly, and stop dropping at what would otherwise be excellent locations because the supplies will almost surely be vandalized. I believe that it is likely that before this woman died, she either passed a drop that had been vandalized or a place where there would have been a drop if it were not for the actions of these agents. I believe that it is very likely that had she found our supplies, she would have survived long enough for us to find her.

As far as I am concerned, the people who are doing this are murderers and her blood is on their hands.[*]

Border Patrol agents really are scared, even if right now they don't actually have much to worry about. It's written all over their faces. I guess destroying people's lives for a living must do that to you. "There are few things under heaven more unnerving than the silent, accumulating contempt and hatred of a people," as James Baldwin put it. Personally, it gives me great pleasure to be able to go unarmed daily to places that people with automatic weapons and body armor are terrified to set foot in. I have not made myself an enemy of the people—and in the long run, that is going to keep me safer than them.

[*] For extensive source material, see the abuse documentation report *Disappeared: How the US Border Enforcement Agencies Are Fueling a Missing Persons Crisis,* released in 2016 by Derechos Humanos and No More Deaths.

In 2012, we caught Border Patrol red-handed destroying resources we put out for migrants in distress. At our wits' end at their constant vandalism, we began to hide cameras in places where we knew they would destroy supplies. Within a matter of days, we had a video of a smiling blonde Border Patrol agent kicking down a line of water bottles in the middle of the summer, and of another using a racial epithet to boot. The epithet was *tonk,* in everyday use within Border Patrol to refer to migrants; the word is derived from the sound a flashlight makes when you use it to hit someone over the head.

The footage debuted on the PBS program "Need To Know" and circulated widely on the internet. The government looked *bad.* It did not go well with the administration's efforts to pander to the Latino vote leading up to the 2012 presidential elections, and somebody up the food chain told agents in the field to knock it off. This simple action cost us $75, and led to a marked decrease in vandalism in the Arivaca sector that lasted until after the elections.

This episode illustrated a truism that is also applicable to those trying to stop the police from killing Black people: only negative reinforcement will work on these people. If killing people has no negative impact on the personal or professional well-being of individual rank-and-file members of law enforcement, they will go on doing it forever. Changing law enforcement behavior means finding a way to exert enough leverage to bring about these consequences. We did this one way, teenagers in Ferguson did it another.

What's good for the goose is good for the gander: deterrence is a two-way street. *The hills have eyes, you cowards.*

The Game

It's reasonable to hate everyone involved in the business of human trafficking on both sides of the law and border. The people at the bottom of the food chain usually end up doing the dirtiest work. "Love the soldier, hate the war," as the saying goes; "Love the player, hate the game." It's hard to say. Love the sinner; hate the sin? I don't know.

The teenage boy from Sonora who leaves the teenage girl from Honduras to die in the desert is a black pawn. The Border Patrol agent who scattered his group and put him in that position is a white knight. You know this metaphor. They are all responsible for their actions, but somebody else set up the board.

There's a game beyond the game, and it's clear who's winning. The players don't have to sit at the same table; they play into each other's hands.

I worked in the desert for seven years. The Minutemen had no compassion, no vision, and no soul, but in some ways they were right: if the government wanted to shut down drug smuggling and human trafficking on the border, they probably could. They won't. There's too much money at stake: American politicians, Mexican politicians, Border Patrol, cartels, local police, state police, federal police, private security, DEA, FBI, SWAT teams, banks, employers, bail bondsmen, lawyers, public defenders, district attorneys, judges, courts, county jails, state prisons, federal prisons, private prisons, weapons manufacturers, erectors of towers, builders of walls. Total surveillance infrastructure; eternal war profiteering; the corporate state. The whole thing is a sick charade. They'll never cut the head off of the golden goose. Don't bet on it. I'm done playing games with them.

The Desert

The desert is full of trash. Water bottles, tin cans, food wrappers, backpacks, blankets, shoes, socks, pants, shirts, hats, maxipads, toilet paper . . . there must be hundreds of millions of tons of the stuff. Anti-immigrant trolls love to talk about it. This is not because they actually care about the environment, but because they hope to confuse people who sympathize with migrants. It's like Bush taking a sudden interest in the position of women in Afghan society back in 2001. You don't hear these people talk very much about the border wall obstructing wildlife migration patterns, or about the huge swaths of public land that are being leased out by the government to giant mining and ranching companies for a pittance, or about the depletion of the watershed as a result of cattle and urban sprawl.

Unlike these characters, I actually care about the desert and have done my best to clean it up. I've hauled countless truckloads of garbage out of there, which is more than almost anyone on the opposing side can say. I tell new volunteers that as soon as they've picked up their first bottle, they've done more to deal with the problem than 99.99% of the Border Patrol agents, Game and Fish wardens, Fish and Wildlife officers, militia members, and armchair quarterbacks watching right-wing pundits on TV ever have or will. Border militarization has pushed migrant traffic into the wilderness, and consequently it's getting trashed. If you don't like that, then we need to figure out some way to stop the border militarization.

There is nowhere on earth like the Sonoran Desert. It is beautiful beyond telling: wild, harsh, vast, mountainous, remote, rugged, unforgiving, everything you can think of and more. Many times that I felt weak, like I was going to lose my mind, I turned to its inhabitants for strength: the deer, jackrabbit, kangaroo mouse, stinkbug, tarantula, tortoise, rattlesnake, raccoon, ringtail,

"Borders: Scars on the Earth"

– anonymous graffiti on the south side
of the border wall, Nogales, Sonora

coatimundi, pronghorn, javelina,* raven, vulture, eagle, coyote, mountain lion, panther, ocotillo, catclaw, shindagger, prickly pear, barrel cactus, cholla, saguaro, and even some of the cows, dogs, cats, and people. I could find our camp from anywhere between the Baboquivaris and the Atascosas; on foot, from memory, every time, without fail. I located myself between those mountains for a season of my life.

The desert is full of places that are sacred to me. There is the last place I saw Esteban, the place I found Alberto, the places where Claudia and José and Susana and Roberto died, Jamie's rock, Yolanda's hill and Alfredo's tree. It is overwhelming to think that as many of the stories as I know—as many as anyone will ever know—that is just a drop in the bucket of all that has happened there. The objects that people leave behind are a constant reminder of this to me, a physical manifestation of all of the best and worst that human beings have to offer. I am not a particularly spiritual person, but the weight of these remnants is immense and often oppressive.

I love the desert. It breaks my heart that it has played host to such terrible suffering. It gives me some solace to know that someday—even if it is only because there are no more human beings left on the planet—there will be no more United States, no more Mexico, no more helicopters, no more walls, no Border Patrol and no border. The plastic will break down, the memory of these things will fade, and the land will finally have a chance to heal under the blue sky and the merciless sun.

* A word about the javelina. They have mohawks, a musky aroma, and large sharp tusks protruding from their faces; they live in extended matrilineal groups, raise each other's young, become dangerous when cornered, appear to operate by consensus, and will eat anything that is not nailed down. They are the punks of the desert. Even where everything else is desperate, they seem to have life all figured out.

The North

"You haven't heard
our thunder yet!"

*– slogan at a protest
against SB1070,
Tucson, Arizona, 2010*

Immigrants

The corporate, governmental, and criminal elites that benefit from the suffering on the border are ruthless and powerful, but they are not gods. They aren't the only actors in this drama, and they don't have the situation completely under control. People make it through the desert because they are brave and resourceful, not just because the Border Patrol lets them. The trails themselves are extraordinary testaments to human ingenuity, weaving gracefully through canyons and over mountains with an unerring eye for direction and cover.

There are nearly twelve million undocumented people in this country. Working in the desert has underscored for me that they are not all the same. The migrants are not all angels, or devils, or victims. They are not passive objects that are acted upon by the world without acting in return. They are complex individuals who have chosen to take their lives into their own hands, and I have chosen to take their side as best I can. Sometimes it works out and sometimes it doesn't. Sometimes you beat the man and sometimes the man beats you.

We were walking up a small canyon. One of my companions was doing very loud and rather florid call outs: "¡COMPAÑERAS! ¡COMPAÑEROS! ¡NO TENGAN MIEDO! ¡TENEMOS AGUA, COMIDA, Y MEDICAMENTOS! ¡SOMOS AMIGOS! ¡NO SOMOS LA MIGRA! ¡ESTAMOS AQUÍ PARA AYUDARLES! ¡SI NECESITAN CUALQUIER COSA: *GRITENOS*!" The great majority of the time, no one is there to hear these call outs.

We turned a corner in the canyon, and there were about thirty-five people: men, women, children, and teenagers, dressed all in blacks, browns, and desert tans, dead silent and taking up a very small amount of space. "Holy shit! Uh, did you hear us coming?"

"Yes, we heard you coming." It was very hot. We gave them lots of water, food, socks, and treated a number of blisters and sprained ankles. They were all from Guatemala. They said they had been together every step of the way. As we prepared to part ways, one of them handed us a large sack of money—pesos, quetzales, and dollars.

"Um, no, you don't understand, you don't have to give us any money, this is why we are here."

"No, it's you who does not understand," he said. "We found this money at a shrine in the desert. We decided that it was not doing anybody any good there, so we took it. If the migra catch us they will take it from us, and it will never do anybody any good. We want you to take this money, and to use it to help other migrants." We carried out their wishes.

The border doesn't end at the border, and the hardships that undocumented people face don't stop there either. The border cuts through every city and state; it cuts through many of our own bodies. The line in the sand is neither the first nor the last twist of the meat grinder that global capitalism has prepared for people without papers.

After crossing the border, undocumented people enter a world in which they cannot legally earn money. They have compelling reasons not to call an ambulance, go to the hospital, obtain health or automobile insurance, drive a vehicle, open a bank account, use a credit card, apply for a mortgage, sign a lease, or rely on any number of other options that people with citizenship can fall back on. If for any reason you have made it a practice to live a portion of your life off the books, you might be able to appreciate how hard it is to do so full time in this society.

The most telling term in the lexicon of migration in North America is *pollo*. I avoid the word like the plague, but it's widely used by everyone involved in the human trafficking industry on both sides of the law and border, from the top on down. Undocumented people are "*pollos*"—walking meat. It's perfect. If marijuana smugglers are used as beasts of burden, migrants and refugees are driven like cattle to the slaughter. All are hunted like wild game.

Here the thing, though: people will not be treated like animals. Actually, animals will not be treated like animals either, not if they can help it. Anyone who has ever had to reason with a recalcitrant donkey or flee from an angry bull can attest to this.

Undocumented people are indeed the victims of this story, but they are also the victors. They are subject to forces beyond their control, but they are also the subject of history.

For millions of people worldwide, illegal immigration is a legitimate form of resistance to the iniquities of global capitalism. It is the most effective action that many people can take to change the conditions in which they live. It may be indirect resistance, but it gets the goods in two specific ways.

First, it is effective economically. Remittances from immigrant workers in the United States—many of them undocumented—to their families in Mexico totaled more than 24.8 billion dollars in 2015 alone, plus 6.25 billion from Guatemalans, 4.28 billion from Salvadorans, and 3.4 billion from Hondurans. If you add up all the remittances from immigrant workers in the entire global north to all of their families in the entire global south, the total starts to look pretty significant. It's filtered through a fine screen of work and exploitation; but all the same, this money represents one of the largest redistributions of wealth from the rich to the poor in the entire course of human history. This is a big deal in the here and now.

Second, it is effective demographically. South-to-north immigration, much of it illegal, is bringing about real demographic shifts in parts of the global north and particularly in the United States. This shift may eventually lead to meaningful changes within this country, which could contribute to a somewhat more equitable restructuring of the global economic system, which would mitigate the tremendous disparity in wealth between the global north and south—which is what drives the migration in the first place.

It's certainly not a given that this latter hope will pan out. Generations of immigrants have moved from the margins into the mainstream of American society without radically changing its character. In fact, this is exactly how settlers took control of the land to begin with. Nonetheless, a distinctive feature of American history is that this pathway has generally been reserved

for immigrants of European ancestry. It has not yet been proven that this country can assimilate or segregate the current influx of non-European immigrants without eventually undermining the foundation of white supremacy upon which it has been built.

We got a call from our neighbors. A man had crawled up to their door. He was in terrible shape. He could barely stand or talk. He had not eaten or drunk water for three days, and he hadn't urinated for a day and a half. It had been deadly hot. We tried to give him fluids, but he would vomit immediately every time.

"This is really bad," I told him. "You need an IV. We don't have one here. You may have kidney damage. We can't treat that. You need to go to the hospital. They will deport you after they treat you, but if you don't I am really afraid that you might die."

"No," he said. "Don't call them."

"Please, I understand, but—"

"No. Don't call them."

"But—"

"No." We laid him down. After several hours, he managed to keep down a tiny amount of water. We nursed him through the night as best we could, giving him water every hour or so. By morning, he was able to hold it down without vomiting, and he finally urinated a little bit. He could barely sit up, but he was able to talk again.

"I've never seen anyone so sick refuse to go to the hospital," I said. "What happened to you?"

"I've lived in the states for eighteen years," he told us. "I've never been in any trouble. I've never even gotten a parking ticket. My wife and I finally paid off our house. All my children are here. So are my grandchildren. For work, I take care of elderly people. Six months ago, I had an accident and I broke my back. I was in bed for nearly four months. I was working again, and I got pulled over. The policeman said that I didn't use my turn signal. I've been here eighteen years and I never got pulled over once. I've always been very careful. They sent me to a detention facility. They kept me there for fifteen days, with chains on my hands

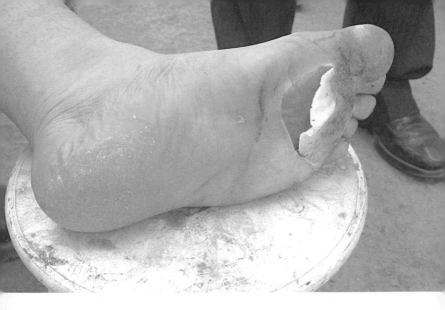

and feet. They fed us peanut butter crackers three times a day. I was shackled the whole time. They dropped me off across the border with nothing. I had nowhere to go. I hadn't been there in so long. I left with a group that night. They drove us way out into the desert. We walked for three days. I couldn't keep up any longer. I'm not a young man any more. They left me out there with no food or water. I was by myself for three more days. I had no idea where I was. I drank dirty water from a cattle pond, and it made me even sicker. I was hearing voices and seeing things. When I saw that house up there, I didn't know if it was real or not. I kept walking towards it. I thought that I might have already died. I can't do this again. My whole life is here. There is nothing for me in this world if I can't make it back. If I die, I die. This is my only chance. I have to keep trying."

He recovered slowly. He called us from his house a week after he left. A month later, he and his wife sent down a huge package of shoes and food and clothing to give to other migrants. "I almost always stay inside," he said. "I can't afford to risk being sent back again. I suffered so much out there. I'm still healing. I know that I could never make it another time."

Citizens

The impending demographic change in the United States is a cause of real anxiety for some powerful Americans, as well as many less powerful ones who have not managed to think all the way through its ramifications. As far as I'm concerned, the sooner it comes, the better. In my opinion, even a partial erosion of white supremacy in the United States is actually in the long-term self-interest of most "white" Americans such as myself.

You can build a throne out of bayonets, but you can't sit on it long.

Aside from the fact that subjugating other people is a rotten thing to do, it's not a very safe way to live. It's extraordinarily impressive that Black people in the United States managed to break free from both slavery and Jim Crow without resorting to indiscriminate slaughter of white people on a grand scale. It certainly would have been understandable to do so, and it arguably would have been justified. I suspect that things would have been much uglier if there had not been at least a few white people who were willing to do the right thing. I don't know if I want to bet that the billions of people that are being pushed around the world today will be so restrained when it comes time to pay the piper on a global level. It seems better to get on the winning side while there still may be time.[*]

In any case, the wheels are coming off the bus. We live on the same small planet as everybody else. The way of life we inherited has proven disastrous for the biosphere and for the long-term prospects of human survival. My generation is perhaps the first group of white Americans that not only have an ethical mandate to turn away from this path, but also an urgent self-interest in doing so. Left unchecked, the current arrangement is guaranteed

---

[*] "I am now quite certain that the crimes of this guilty land will never be purged away but with blood. I had as I now think vainly flattered myself that without very much bloodshed it might be done." -John Brown, on his way to the gallows, December 2, 1859

to cannibalize what is left of our land base within our lifetimes and leave our children with nothing but the bones.[†]

Admittedly, this is complicated. Groups of humans have subjugated other groups of humans and destroyed their own land bases since long before the social construct of whiteness ever existed, and people of European ancestry are not the only ones who are capable of doing either of these things. White supremacy is not the only linchpin holding this all together, but it is a significant one. At this point, I don't think we can hope to stop the devastation of our planet without contesting the structures of white supremacy—or vice versa.

So the answer is not for white Americans to continue to defend the indefensible at the price of our souls, or to crawl into a hole and die. It is for those of us who fit that description to think carefully about where our allegiance really lies, and to find ways to act on it in materially meaningful ways. There are examples throughout history of people who did just this—members of oppressor and colonizer groups who decided to throw in their lot with the colonized and oppressed. You can point to white people involved in the Underground Railroad during slavery, gentiles who sheltered Jews during the Holocaust, white Americans who took part in the civil rights movement, white South Africans who resisted Apartheid, Americans involved in the Sanctuary movement during the wars in Central America in the 1980s, and Israelis resisting the occupation of Palestine today, to name a few. It's a good story to be part of. Those of us who are positioned to do so should embrace it and be proud of it.

Our opponents will call us traitors, as if we support another government. In fact, we have pledged our allegiance to something older and wiser than anything that any nation-state has to offer,

---

† "It is a written fact that our people had warned of all these consequences of wrongful environmental behavior since our very first contact with the non-Indians. There was a time when our elders used to say to us, 'You can't function with one foot in the white man's canoe and one foot in the Indian's canoe.' With these extreme environmental concerns taking place on the earth, mankind is all in the same boat. Or better be." – Leonard Peltier

> # *"Las paredas vueltas de lado son puentes."*
> # (Walls turned sideways are bridges.)
>
> *– graffiti quoting Angela Davis on the south side of the border wall, Nogales, Sonora*

and it is the apologists for the current order who have turned their backs and lost their way.[*]

Working on the border has shown me time and again that you can't really extricate one part of the equation from all the other parts. Once you start untangling one thread, you find that it's tied into a noose wrapped around your own neck. The drug war will not end without structural change throughout Mexico, which will not happen without structural change in Colombia and the other cocaine-producing countries, which will not happen without structural change in the United States, and so on. You can reverse the order of these statements or add others and they will still be true. So, for example, fighting internal deportations

[*] "I never have lost sight of what human potential there is in people. This is at the heart of what motivates me—my intent, my purpose, my goals, my values, this is where it's at. It's my commitment. This is what the government fears. That I didn't go back to that mill to make those shoe heels, that I took another course with my life. I have a commitment to a future that holds the human potential of poor and working class people as a great asset to be developed. A commitment to a future in which no child will ever have to suffer from racism, poverty, or war. A future where justice brings peace for our children and generations to come." – Raymond Luc Levasseur, facing life in prison, in his closing remarks to the jury, United States Courthouse, Springfield, MA, January 10, 1989. See the 2015 documentary *An American* by Pierre Marier.

and fighting border militarization are not two distinct projects.

This has global implications, but it is especially true in the case of Mexico, the United States, and their devil-child The Border. Nothing will get better on the border without things changing in both countries, and the problems in one country will not be solved without addressing the problems in the other.

Once, I asked this Oaxacan guy what he thought it would take to end the death in the desert. "*Una revolución binacional,*" he answered, without hesitating. We laughed, because of course that is impossible. For now.

New volunteers sometimes ask me what I think a just border policy would look like. I tell them that there is no such thing; it is a contradiction in terms. I am not interested in helping the authorities figure out how to fix the mess they've created. Ultimately, the only hope for a solution to the border crisis lies in bringing about worldwide systemic change that ensures freedom of movement for all people, rejects the practice of state control over territory, honors indigenous autonomy and sovereignty, addresses the legacies of slavery and colonization, equalizes access to resources between the global north and the global south, and fundamentally changes human beings' relationship to the planet and all of the other forms of life that inhabit it. That's a tall order! Where to start?

The desert is not the only place, but it is one. The strength of our work is that there is no doubt we are having a tangible effect on the lives of individual people who find our water, our food, or us. I know many people who I am certain would have died were it not for the resources that we offered, and many more who made it back to their families that never would have been able to do so without meeting us. I don't say this to pat myself on the back, but to say that it is possible to start somewhere.

People sometimes lament the fact that it can feel like we are just serving as a band-aid. This word always aggravates me, because the stakes are too high and the metaphor is not strong enough. One life means a lot to the person who lives it. "Tourniquet," I tell them. "You mean you don't want us to just serve as a tourniquet."

Nevertheless, the weakness of our work is that we are always dealing with the symptoms and never the cause. It can feel like we're always cleaning up a mess we didn't create, like a child trying to mend the damage an abusive parent is doing to the rest of the family. It's better than nothing, but what we really need to do is to stop the abuse.

Many of the most effective types of direct action can end up looking like some version of damage control.* The problem is that it's easier to make attainable goals and quantify success when dealing with individuals than when dealing with a system. I can visualize the steps from A to Z of how to drop twenty-five gallons of water on a trail. When I wake up in the morning, there is always something that I can do to move towards that goal. I have a much harder time visualizing how to get Border Patrol out of the desert, and a harder time still imagining how to effectuate structural economic change on a global scale. It can be tempting to say that it's better to succeed at what we can do than fail at what we can't, but that's just defeatism. I really don't want to be doing these same water drops twenty-five years from now. So what should we do?

Thankfully, none of us has to do everything. It's not my job to act like Moses and set the people free. That's not how meaningful social change happens. I can do my best to help, but if people are going to get free they are going to do it themselves. I simply can't call the shots in other people's struggles for liberation. I trust that the millions of people who are most directly affected by immigration and border enforcement will keep finding ways to combat it. There will almost certainly be things that white US citizens can do if we keep our ears to the ground. If my efforts in the desert are in any way contributing to 39 billion dollars moving from the rich to the poor every year, then I'm happy.

* See *Down With Empire, Up With Spring,* published anonymously in England in 2003 by the Do or Die collective. For a practical example animated by biocentric ethics in the arena of wilderness defense, see Blue Mountains Biodiversity Project at bluemountainsbiodiversityproject.org. There are countless other such examples in every arena of struggle.

Ulises limped into camp with his full weight on a tree branch, dragging his right leg behind him.

"Is your leg broken?" we asked him. He was young and skinny.

"No," he answered. "I only *have* one leg. My prosthetic foot is broken."

Sure enough, his leg was amputated above the knee. He had walked all the way from Altar, six days over the mountains. His foot had finally given out on the fourth day. I had never seen anything like this.

"Whoa, dude."

I knew a guy that knew a guy, and I made some phone calls.

"We need a *foot,*" I told him. "With a *quickness.*"

Two days later, there was a package waiting in Tucson. Inside it was a foot.

I drove back to camp, and Ulises was doing the dishes. There was a group of twelve men in the kitchen.

"I don't trust these guys," he told me, under his breath. "Some of these dudes are shifty. I haven't told them I've only got one leg. They think it's broken or something. We've got to switch it out in the trailer where they can't see." He was limping terribly.

I got the package from the truck, and the twelve men watched us walk into the small pop-up trailer.

Ulises had an Allen key to loosen the screw that held on his foot. We both pried on it, but the screw was rusted solidly in place.

"Fuck," he said. "We need some WD-40."

I got some out of the truck, in front of the twelve men. He sprayed it around the screw until the trailer filled up with fumes. We both pried and pried, but it would not budge.

"Mother *fucker,*" he said. "We need a ratchet set."

I got one out of the truck, and the twelve men watched me return to the trailer. No matter what we did, the screw would not move.

"Motherfucking son a *bitch*!" he said. "We need a pipe!"

I found a long pipe, in front of the twelve men.

He put the pipe over the ratchet handle. We braced against each other and pulled.

The screw broke free!

Ulises slammed the new foot into place and tightened everything down. He started to pace in circles inside the tiny trailer.

"Oh yeah, this is a *good* one. I'm good to go. I'm good to *go!*"

He then stomped out of the trailer and back into the kitchen to finish the dishes, walking quickly and confidently. I can only imagine what it must have looked like to the twelve men. By all appearances, I had laid hands on him in the trailer, and healed his broken leg with WD-40, a ratchet set, and a pipe. They left later that evening.

Ulises was from Chiapas.

"Man, look," he told me over dinner. "My town fucking sucks. There's only two things in my town: bananas and dead people. I'm not kidding. Look up the front page of the newspaper if you don't believe me. Bananas and dead people. That's what you'll see. The mafias are killing everybody down there. Anyway, I was seeing this girl, right? I was really in love with her. We'd been together for a long time. We were going to get married and everything. But I didn't have any money, and I didn't want to work on the banana plantation, and I didn't want to work for the mafia, and there's nothing else you can do down there. So I went to Mexico City, to make some money, so that we could get married. And I saved up a bunch of money, and I went back home, and she had gotten married to this other dude!"

"Oh, man," I said.

"And *then,*" he continued, "well, I was pretty sad. So I was at this party, and I was dancing with this other girl, and well, you know, I got her pregnant. She's due in two months."

"Hmm..."

"But we barely know each other, right? She doesn't want to be with me, I don't want to be with her. Her parents are *pissed.* They fucking hate me. They don't want her to have anything to do with me. And meanwhile, I can't even walk around town without seeing the girl that I really love, and she's with this other guy. So I was like, you know what? I'm done with this place. I'm going to the United States. I'll send money home to my son when he's born, and maybe when he grows up he won't have to pick bananas or kill somebody for the mafia."

"Damn."

Pretty soon I realized that Ulises was really, really smart. Sharp. Sharp like only one-legged teenagers from violent and depressing small towns in southern Mexico can be. He was incredibly observant, and he remembered everything. When he was ready to leave, we walked up the hill above camp. It was blazingly hot. He was going to walk to Tucson, four more days at least.

I told him everything I knew; the *arroyos*, mountains, hills, landmarks, time, distance, north, south, east, west, everything from Mexico to Phoenix. No small amount of information. He nodded grimly, without saying a word. When I was done he repeated it all back to me, succinctly and accurately, with a few cogent questions thrown in. I knew he was going to make it. Within a week, he sent word that he was at his uncle's house in Oakland.

I looked up the paper from his hometown. Bananas and dead people on the front page.

Things didn't work out with his uncle. Ulises needed somewhere to stay. He ended up living with old friends of mine, and he would regularly send me hilarious updates about their punk bands and four-dimensional love lives. He seemed happy.

Six months later, the mother of his son was murdered in his hometown. Ulises dropped everything and flew home to Chiapas to help her mother raise the baby. I lost touch with him, as did everyone I knew. I always wondered what happened to him.

One day, five years later, I was in Tucson, and I got a message from camp.

"You've got to come down here. There's a guy with one leg asking about you by name. He walked in with a Honduran family. A thirteen-year-old girl, a seventeen-year-old boy, and a fifty-five-year-old man. You should have seen him, he threw his hat down on the ground and started jumping around and waving his arms and was like, 'I knew it! I knew it! I told you we'd make it! I knew we could find this place!'"

I drove out to camp. I could not believe my eyes.

"Ulises! *Ulises!* What *happened?*" He had filled out a little, and he didn't look like a kid anymore.

"Listen, man," he told me. "My son is with his grandmother. We get along pretty well now. We decided that it would be best for me to come back here to work. I went up to Altar and got with a group. We got split up by a chopper just north of the border, same shit as always, and the fucking guide ran off like usual. I got away with these three Hondurans. I told them 'Look, there's this place somewhere out here where they'll help us. We can get food and water and medicine and sleep. It's been five years, and I'm not exactly sure where we are, but I think I can find it. If you want to come with me, you can.' We spent six days in the mountains. I spent every minute of it thinking about that conversation we had on the hill up there. I tried to remember every word you said. I was thinking so hard that smoke was coming out of my ears. We went in circles a little bit, but we made it. We walked right down the driveway. I did it, man. I found you guys again."

I am still in awe of Ulises. He found our camp in the vast expanse of the Sonoran Desert, from memory, after five years, without a phone or a map or a GPS, and he led three people to safety who otherwise easily could have died. Not one person in a million would have been willing and able to do that. The Border Patrol can pin as many medals to their chests as they feel like, and these politicians can wrap themselves in the flag. Whatever. Ulises is a *real* American hero. He's working in the United States now, sending money home to his son.

Resistance

With that caveat, dear reader—that none of us has to do everything—please permit me to address you directly. The death in the desert is not the only messed up thing in the world. But it is pretty bad, and it hits close to home for me. I would really like to see it end. I encourage you to find a way to get involved. I can't tell you exactly how to do this. Coming to work in the desert is one way. There are many others. There are communities of undocumented people in nearly every part of the country, if not the world. What is the situation in your area, and what might you have to offer? There are institutions that benefit from this whole catastrophe in nearly every part of the country, as well. What might you be able to do?

Some have suggested[*] that in order to link systemic change with tangible goals, we must find points of intervention in the system where we can apply power to leverage transformation. These points of intervention include the point of production, the point of destruction, the point of consumption, the point of decision, and the point of assumption. It's not perfect, but it's as good a framework as any to use when thinking about how to intervene in this particular situation.

What might direct action at the point of production look like? Stalling the construction of new CCA facilities? What about at the point of destruction? Finding ways to interfere with BP/ICE operations or intervene in deportations? What about the point of consumption? Pressuring businesses to commit to non-compliance with anti-immigrant laws and organizing boycotts of ones that refuse? The point of decision? Interrupting meetings or legislative processes? What might direct action at the point of assumption look like? What lies and assumptions are used to justify the dehumanization of immigrants? How might you be able to counter them? Do you have other ideas?

Direct action in the context of humanitarian aid in the desert is a relatively new field, all things considered. There are many tactics yet to be developed, and many proven tactics that have not been pushed to their limits. There is still much to learn and much that new people can offer. Most promisingly, the trans-national, cross-cultural, and inter generational alliances that have been forged in the crucible of the border have yet to approach their full potential. Our ability to realize this potential will determine the extent of the success of our campaign to end migrant deaths in the desert, as well as whether that campaign ever develops into a deeper resistance to the systems at the root of the problem. They haven't heard our thunder yet.

* Patrick Reinsborough and Doyle Canning in "Points of Intervention," for example.

I don't generally get too excited about actions in which people get arrested on purpose. "That goes against all my hustling ethics," says Lupe Fiasco, and I usually agree. Civil disobedience is widely fetishized in the United States, even though it does not always produce the most desirable results. However, like any other tactic, it can be quite effective under the right circumstances.

For example, on October 11, 2013, two groups of people chained themselves to two G4S (formerly Wackenhut) buses full of 70 detainees headed for "Operation Streamline" hearings at the federal courthouse in Tucson, Arizona. Another group chained themselves together inside the courthouse itself. This story requires some context.

Operation Streamline is a joint initiative of the Department of Homeland Security and Department of Justice, started in 2005, that adopts a zero-tolerance approach to unauthorized border crossing. In contrast to previous policy, immigration violations are processed under the criminal justice system. First-time offenders are prosecuted for misdemeanor illegal entry, which carries a six-month maximum sentence. Anyone who has been deported in the past and is caught re-entering can be charged with felony re-entry, which carries a two-year sentence but can involve up to a 20-year maximum if the person has a criminal record. Over 99% of people "streamlined" plead guilty, because those who do so are likely to get shorter prison terms, whereas those who don't are likely to get close to the maximum sentence.

Another distinguishing feature is that cases are not heard individually, but rather are processed in one large group. A single case in the Tucson courthouse can include up to 70 defendants. The group cases typically take from 30 minutes to two and a half hours to decide, meaning from 25 seconds to 2 minutes per defendant. Furthermore, defense attorneys are typically afforded no longer than 30 minutes per client for consultations, which take place on the morning of the trial. These consultations are held in the open—in the very same courtroom that will later hold the en masse trial. This is all of dubious legality at best, but they've been happily doing it every business day for years. Business is good.

Bear in mind that people are regularly sent to prison for years in these kangaroo courts. I'm no fan of legal proceedings, period—but even by normal standards, Streamline is a travesty of justice. Strictly speaking, it's a failure of due process. The clear objective of all of this is to pull more people into the legal system. The end result is that tens of millions of taxpayer dollars are funneled to the private prison industry that will warehouse the detainees—to G4S, for example.

Streamline was brought to a full stop in Tucson on the day of the bus action. It took the police long enough to figure out how to deal with the situation that all hearings for the day had to be canceled. There was then no way to bring the detainees back in for trial, because the court had 70 more people booked for the next day, and the next, and the next, on into infinity. All detainees on both buses were eventually deported without criminal prosecution, because the government was unable to provide them a speedy trial under the letter of the law. The government then tried but ultimately failed to convict the participants in the action of various charges. The defendants in the case were eventually sentenced to 14 hours in jail: time served, no fines.

There is some disagreement about the efficacy of the action, however, because an abnormally high percentage of the detainees were then laterally deported. For context, lateral deportation is another questionably legal practice that the government has been engaged in for years. The idea is to send a deportee not to the closest border city to the place they were apprehended, but to somewhere very far away. The Department of Homeland Security was especially fond of delivering people to northeastern Mexico in the early 2010s, when it was basically a war zone. Being laterally deported from Nogales to Matamoros in those years was a bit like getting picked up for a drunk in public charge in San Francisco and being dropped off in Baghdad at midnight after having been relieved of your wallet.

Because of this, some people argued that the negative impacts of the G4S lockdown outweighed the positive ones. Others weren't convinced that the two events were related; still others pointed out that for every action, there is an equal and opposite reaction, and there's no way around this.

As far as I know, however, most people do agree on this: at the end of the day, 70 people were never criminally prosecuted who otherwise certainly would have been, meaning that up to 70 people never went to prison who otherwise were headed directly there.

So the action cost its participants very little and the benefits were great. That's a good outcome. The tactic could easily be replicated or improved upon by people into this sort of thing. Eventually, the law of diminishing returns would kick in—police tactics would improve, fines and sentences would increase, the definition of a speedy trial would change, and so on—but it would be effective for a while. When it ceased to be effective, the participants could develop alternatives, and the battleground would move again.

I'll conclude with two points. First, supply chain management is always at the heart of military logistics. Longer and more complex supply chains are always more susceptible to disruption, and the supply chain of the American government's one-sided war on undocumented people is long and complex indeed, and highly susceptible to disruption. Second, it is possible to assess the effectiveness of most actions by running a simple cost-benefit analysis: how can we get the maximum output, benefit, or payout for the minimum input, risk, or cost? The bus lockdown was a good example of this going well. There is an infinite field of possibility awaiting further experimentation.

"*Vivir para ser libres o morir para dejar de ser esclavos.*"
(Live to be free or die to no longer be slaves.)

– graffiti quoting Práxedis Guerrero on the south side of the border wall, Nogales, Sonora

. . . end up everywhere:

From
East
to
West

This is the best I can do to tell the story of irregular migration in North America. This story is not unique to the United States, or even to the West. Variations on it can be found wherever comparative poverty and instability meet comparative wealth and stability: from Haiti into the Dominican Republic, from the many countries of West Africa through Morocco into Spain at Ceuta and Melilla, from both West Africa and East Africa (Somalia, Eritrea, Sudan, South Sudan) through Libya and across the Mediterranean Sea into Italy at Lampedusa, from East Africa over the Sinai Peninsula into Israel, from the Central African Republic to anywhere else, from southern Africa (especially Zimbabwe) into South Africa, from the Middle East (Syria, Iraq) and Central Asia (Afghanistan, Pakistan) through Turkey and across the eastern Mediterranean into Greece at Lesbos, from Bangladesh into India, from both Bangladesh and Myanmar (especially of Rohingya people) over the Andaman Sea and into Southeast Asia (Malaysia, Thailand, Indonesia), from South Asia (India, Pakistan, Bangladesh, Sri Lanka, Nepal) and the Philippines into the Gulf states (through the *kafala* system), from North Korea across China and Laos into Thailand and then South Korea, from rural China to urban China (owing to the *hukou* system), and from various parts of Asia and the Middle East through Indonesia and over the Timor Sea into Australia... to name just a few examples.

Any one of these routes could fill a book. Every place is different, but the story is always the same. Everywhere there is the same border. Everywhere people die to cross it, confronting the same barriers and guards. Everywhere there is the same human trafficking industry built up around it, with the same patterns of kidnapping, extortion, indentured servitude, slavery, and rape. Everything is blamed on these traffickers, who are not the cause of the problem but a byproduct of it. Everywhere there is unequal exchange: high prices, low wages, and chaos on one side; high wages, low prices, and order on the other. Everywhere there is the same hyper-exploitation of undocumented labor in the interior, the same terror of deportation, the same profiteering off of detention and border militarization, and the same scapegoating of migrants and refugees. Everywhere there is the same attempt to outsource the problem to buffer states (Mexico, Morocco, Libya, Turkey, Indonesia), the same third-party deportations, the same leveraging of displaced people to negotiate concessions between these states and the states that call the shots in the first world—between the periphery and the core.* Everywhere there is surplus humanity, who refuse to disappear even though capitalism has no use for them.

Increasingly, there is only one option left, one place left to turn, one employer still hiring: pure nihilism. ISIS, Boko Haram, the Zetas. Warlords. Even when every single door is closed, the excluded can still hire on according to this principle: "If our lives are worth nothing, then nothing is sacred." This is not the world in which I want to live.

The core tenet of "free trade," the globalized capitalism that has dominated the world since the end of the Cold War, is that capital should be able to move freely across borders, while labor and surplus humanity are constrained by them. The state's primary role—increasingly, its *only* role—is to police the interior and guard the border. Citizenship has become the primary determinant in a multi-layered global caste system. After more than 25 years, this system appears to be operating less and less smoothly. It may be breaking down altogether.[†]

* The overwhelming majority (86%) of people defined as refugees under international law are hosted in so-called "developing countries" such as Turkey, Lebanon, Jordan, Pakistan, Iran, Ethiopia, and Kenya, among others—not in Western Europe, the United States, or elsewhere in the first world. As of 2016, Lebanon is hosting 1.5 million Syrian refugees, who now constitute a quarter of the Lebanese population—far and away the highest ratio of refugees to citizens anywhere in the world. At equivalent levels, the United States would be hosting 107 million refugees. See *Global Trends: Forced Displacement in 2015.*

† As of the end of 2015, the UN Refugee Agency reports that 65.3 million people were forcibly displaced worldwide as a result of persecution, conflict, generalized violence, and human rights violations. According to the report, this is 5.8 million more than just 12 months earlier, and the number of displaced people is now at its highest ever—surpassing even the aftermath of World War II.

"I'm a riot
I'ma riot through your borders
Call me bulletproof"

– Beyoncé Knowles-Carter, "Freedom," 2016

I'm opposed to all borders and in favor of the free movement of all people across the face of the earth. I don't think that the practice of regulating movement according to place of birth is justifiable under any coherent ethical, philosophical, spiritual, or even legal system.

Mind you, I'm not a utopian. I don't think there is any chance that borders will magically cease to exist, or that there would be no undesirable side effects if they did. However, any step in that direction is better than nothing. There are a few places where irregular migration is managed in a comparatively humane fashion, such as from Nicaragua into Costa Rica, from Syria into Lebanon, or from Bolivia, Paraguay, and Peru into Argentina and Brazil.

Relaxing or abolishing the borders would produce new problems. But unless we believe that certain lives are more valuable than others, then from the standpoint of what will do the most good for the most people, we would be better off facing these problems directly, courageously, and as soon as possible. Yes, it would make it easier for terrorists to attack the West—but if the West ceased to be a sealed fortress sucking in resources, there would be less incentive to attack it. Yes, wars might spread—but like it or not, these wars are already on their way, with a vengeance, and the borders are only exacerbating the conditions that drive people to fight in them.

The writing is on the wall. We live at the end of a time when the needs of certain people could be fulfilled at the expense of others—without a price. That era is drawing to a close.

Chaos and Order

The wall in the desert should be regarded as the symbol of my generation, as surely as the wall in Berlin was the symbol of the last one. Like the Berlin Wall, it will be torn down with hammers and bulldozers. I'll be there if I'm still breathing.

After the end of the Cold War, we were told that we had reached the end of history. The new era was to last forever: liberal democracy, capitalist free trade, US military hegemony, and a carefully managed system of borders to regulate the movement of labor and surplus populations. For a period of time in the 1990s, it was possible for some people to convince themselves that this was true.

Nobody believes this story anymore—least of all the primary beneficiaries of the prevailing order. Their apocalyptic anxiety is written all over their movies, music videos, and advertisements, and especially their contingency plans.* I won't even bother to touch on ecology—*everybody* knows the party can't last, that the carriage turns into a pumpkin at midnight and our children will reap the whirlwind.

At the turn of the century, those of us who opposed the prevailing order understood ourselves as engaged in a bilateral confrontation pitting the interlaced structures of state power and capitalism against the interests of humanity as a whole. I can no longer type those words with a straight face. Another world is always possible, as our slogan proclaimed—but now it's clear that we were not the only ones thinking about what that other world should look like, and that social instability in and of itself is not necessarily a good thing.

So even if the neoliberal era is coming to an end, there are no guarantees that something better will take its place. Those who oppose this order in the name of liberation for all are not the only ones interested in tearing down its borders, nor the best armed,

---

* See *Introduction to the Apocalypse,* published anonymously by the Institute for Experimental Freedom in 2009.

trained, or financed.[†] ISIS may be the first fascist formation in history to be explicitly anti-racist and anti-nationalist. They actually managed to tear down a national border, which is more than any other movement or uprising has accomplished lately.

ISIS miscalculated, of course. People do not tolerate chaos for very long. They look for any possible resolution, including totalitarianism if there is no other option and it isn't possible to escape. People who foment chaos for a living usually want to be the ones in charge. They usually fail. On the other hand, when truly pressed, the people in charge are usually willing to throw society into chaos in order to position themselves as the only way out of it. They often succeed. The old guard have a lot of fight in them still.

This can be seen in both Syria and Mexico. ISIS saved Assad; the Zetas saved the PRI. As of this writing, ISIS is not winning, the Assad regime is. Likewise, the Zetas have lost momentum; Sinaloa and the PRI are more securely in power today than they were ten years ago. Under pressure to transform society (in Mexico by *La Otra Campaña*[‡] in 2006, in Syria by the Arab Spring in 2011), the Syrian and Mexican elites brought on war rather than face revolution. In both cases, the mayhem that followed ultimately served to legitimize their rule. In both cases, it's only a matter of time before social movements reassert themselves to destabilize the existing order from below.

Revolution turns into war. War justifies tyranny. Tyranny leads to revolution.

Rock beats scissors. Scissors cut paper. Paper covers rock.

The stakes of this game are increasingly global. Is there any way to win?

† Furthermore, as the Brexit vote and the election of Donald Trump demonstrate, many of those who oppose this order do so in the name of authoritarian nationalism, and hope to fortify the borders even more heavily than they are now.

‡ See the *Sixth Declaration of the Lacandón Jungle,* issued by the Zapatista Army of National Liberation (EZLN) in June 2005, for a declaration of the principles motivating this ambitious attempt to bring the Zapatista rebellion out of Chiapas and into Mexican society at large.

Transformation

"If there is no struggle there is no progress. Those who profess to favor freedom and yet deprecate agitation are men who want crops without plowing up the ground; they want rain without thunder and lightning. They want the ocean without the awful roar of its many waters. This struggle may be a moral one, or it may be a physical one, and it may be both moral and physical, but it must be a struggle. Power concedes nothing without a demand. It never did and it never will. Find out just what any people will quietly submit to and you have found out the exact measure of injustice and wrong which will be imposed upon them, and these will continue till they are resisted with either words or blows, or with both. The limits of tyrants are prescribed by the endurance of those whom they oppress."

– Frederick Douglass, August 3, 1857

Revolution

Are we talking about a revolution, then? What is revolution? What does it mean?

Marx said it meant seizing the means of production; Lenin said it meant seizing state power. Nechayev said it was the end to justify all means; Stalin said it could happen forever inside the borders of one nation-state. Mao stressed the importance of culture; Pol Pot said it would get us all off to a fresh start. Their dreams were a nightmare, and victory was worse than defeat.

Can this concept be salvaged? I think so. What *is* it?

Bakunin incarnated it; he also predicted how it would turn out if it were misunderstood as a way to put the right people in charge. Red Cloud and Crazy Horse never said a word about it; they didn't have to. Frederick Douglass made a run for it, William Lloyd Garrison argued for it, Harriet Tubman lived for it, and John Brown died for it, though they all called it God. Seth Concklin spent his whole life working for it, and almost nobody ever thanked him or remembered his name. It held out for a week on the barricades of the Paris Commune. Louis Lingg told his captors to hang him for it, and then he beat them to it. Emma Goldman said you can dance to it, Alexander Berkman gave it his best shot, and they kept it together for 47 years. The Wobblies used to ride for it; Mother Jones used to dig it. Durruti said we carry it in our hearts, and that it's growing this minute. In the final month of his life, Malcolm X said that it will ultimately be a global clash between the oppressed and those who do the oppressing—between those who want freedom, justice, and equality for everyone and those who want to continue the systems of exploitation. The Panthers had it all, but their enemies tore it apart: out west the heart, back east the teeth, up north the roots, down south the guts. It scared the hell out of the government all the same. Fred Hampton said it best, and they killed him for it. The Weather Underground tried to set it off. Assata Shakur believed that it could still guide us home to port, and she got away with it. AIM didn't say much about it;

they didn't have to. The Zapatistas stopped talking about it and listened, and then it happened. It is happening again in Rojava, in the most challenging circumstances imaginable.

I caught a glimpse of it in Seattle in 1999 and in Oakland in 2011, but then it slipped away. I'll mostly leave my generation out of it, though: it's not over yet.

One of the founders of No More Deaths once told me a story called "The Parable of the River." It may be familiar to readers who have worked in the non-profit sector or in public health. The framing of the story is not perfect and the metaphor is completely wrong in at least one major way: migrants and refugees are never simply helpless victims, as I hope I have made clear in the preceding text. Most are not babies, and the children grow up fast.[*] Nonetheless, the parable is well known for a good reason. It speaks to the central dilemma of desert aid work and other projects like it.[†]

It goes something like this:

There is a small village on the edge of a river. One day, a villager goes down to the riverbank to wash some clothes. She sees a baby floating down the river! She jumps into the water and pulls the baby to safety. She carries him to the village and finds someone to care for him. Wet and tired, she returns to wash the clothes. She sees another baby floating down the river! Once again, she jumps into the swift current and takes the child into her arms. But before she can climb back onto the riverbank she sees another baby floating towards her. And then another. And

[*] I've watched a lot of interactions between 26-year-old Americans and 16-year-old Hondurans. Generally there is no question as to which one is the adult in the room.

[†] The man who told me the story is well into his eighties. He has been involved in social movements for over fifty years: first in the civil rights movement, then in the movement to end the war in Vietnam, later in the Sanctuary movement, and finally in No More Deaths. He says the story has been around as long as he can remember.

another. She grabs one of them, but she only has two arms. The last two babies float past her. One disappears into the water just out of her reach. The other dashes his head open against a large rock. The woman looks up the river. Six more babies are floating toward her. Horrified, she shouts for help. Villagers working in the field nearby run to help her.

The babies keep coming. Soon, the entire village is occupied with the many tasks that the river demands. There are teams of strong swimmers, who maintain a watch on the riverbank at all times. They pull babies out of the river until their muscles cramp and their teeth are chattering. Sometimes, even the strongest swimmers go into the river once too often. They are swept under by the fierce cold current and their bodies are broken on the rocks. There are people who nurse the babies back to health and tend to their wounds. There are foster parents, carpenters, weavers, gardeners, hunters, teachers, therapists, and cooks. It takes a lot of work to ensure that all of these babies are properly fed, clothed, housed, and integrated into the life of the village. There are people who do *all* of these things and still feel like they are not doing enough.

It is not possible to pull every baby out of the river. Many drown. But the villagers feel that they are doing well to cope with the crisis as best they can. Indeed, the village priest blesses them for their good work. Life goes on.

Eventually, however, it becomes increasingly difficult to provide enough food to feed everyone and to find homes for so many babies. The villagers are exhausted and hungry and sad. Their nerves are shot. Tempers flare. Fights break out. Winter is coming.

One day, two women are seen walking away from the village. "Where are you going?" another villager asks them, disconcerted. "We need you here! Can't you see how busy we are!"

"You all carry on here," says one of the two, machete in hand. The other woman is holding a pitchfork. "We're going upstream to stop whoever is throwing all these babies into the river."

A noisy argument breaks out in the village square.

"It's about time!" roars the blacksmith, raising his hammer.

"Why in the hell didn't we think of that before? We can't afford to go on like this forever. Count me in!" Many of the villagers shout their approval.

"Not so fast!" counters the gravedigger, slamming his pick into the ground. "What will happen if we all just leave our posts? Who will watch the river? Who will care for the children already living among us? Who will staff the clinic, or tend the fields? I'll tell you what will happen. More babies will drown." Many of the same villagers nod in solemn agreement.

"This is a false dichotomy," protests the teenager who washes the dishes. "Some of us should go up the river and some of us should stay here." Most everyone agrees that she has a point, but this is a small village that we are talking about.

"There are not enough of us," says the village priest. "And besides, let's say we decide to head upstream. You grab a shovel and I'll grab an ax. What will we find? Certainly, it's possible that there has been some accident. Perhaps, there is a gaping hole in a bridge somewhere beside a nursery. But that doesn't seem very likely. Given the sheer number of babies in the river, it seems that the most likely explanation is that some hateful or ruthless person is throwing them in. To what end? There must be some reason.

"What will we do if we find the villain? Will we attempt to reason with him and explain why, all things considered, throwing babies in the river is a bad thing to do? Will we push *him* into the river? Are we willing to kill him if that is the only way to end this vile practice?

"What if he is even bigger than our friend the blacksmith? What if he has a gun and is not alone? What if his henchmen are armed with clubs, knives, pistols, shotguns, rifles, heavy artillery, tanks, helicopters, fighter jets, ballistic missiles, and nuclear bombs? How could we ever be able to stop him?"

Thankfully, the priest is missing something and so is this parable. There are millions of people in the river. We have to become capable of helping each other out.

A Hard Lesson

I'm not an uncritical cheerleader for the Zapatistas. However, there's a reason they were able to bring about the first revolution of the post-modern era. They studied their predecessors carefully, applied the lessons that were useful to them, adapted their strategies to their environment, waited patiently until the time was right, acted boldly, and turned the world on its head. As the end of the post-modern era draws near, we should be studying our forebears just as carefully, starting with the Zapatistas themselves.

The Zapatistas broke with all Marxist-Leninist tradition by demonstrating that the seizure of state power was a red herring. They declared war on the Mexican government with no intention of putting themselves in its place. Instead, they focused on establishing autonomous zones. Leftists were profoundly confused, I remember.[*]

Autonomy is the keyword of the Zapatista rebellion.[†] We can define autonomy as the freedom to make decisions and take action in all matters that affect us directly, without seeking permission from a higher power, starting at the level of the individual and scaling up.

It took a year of armed struggle for this concept to fully emerge. Its first appearance in Zapatista canon is in the January 1995 *Third Declaration of the Lacandón Jungle.* By the *Sixth Declaration of the Lacandón Jungle* in June 2005, it was central.

At its core, the Zapatista movement is fighting for indigenous autonomy. By definition, it is both Mexican and Mayan, but

---

[*] I was chicken-hawked by a Trotskyist outfit when I was 14, which was when I first experienced the joy of sects.

[†] In 2002, I was in the autonomous municipality of San Pedro Polhó and there were gaggles of handsome chickens running around everywhere. "Whose chickens are these?" I asked, tellingly. "Oh, they're *autonomous*, they're Zapatistas too," I was told. This is the difference between the voice of the wind from above and the voice of the wind from below: *pollo* versus *autónomo.* The PRI talks about people like they are chickens; the EZLN talks about chickens like they are people.

aims to inspire others to establish autonomous zones elsewhere as well. Zapatistas assert indigenous people's right to self-determination, which has been denied for over 500 years. They argue that the people indigenous to a particular territory should be free to administer their own economy, politics, and resources according to their own traditions and customs. This differs from separatism in that the Zapatistas have been clear that they do not want their own state.

Furthermore, In *El Despertador Mexicano*, on January 1, 1994, the first day of the rebellion, the EZLN defined a right of the people living in Zapatista territory to resist any unjust actions of the EZLN itself, saying that people should "acquire and possess arms to defend their persons, families, and property... against armed attacks committed by the revolutionary forces or those of the government."* This is the acid test. Revolutionaries who claim a monopoly on force the way that the state does are not to be trusted. When you see that, run away as fast as you can.

On the scale of society, autonomy might be understood as the ability to hold territory plus a decentralized and participatory decision-making process to administer it, minus a monopoly on force. Revolution can be pictured as the bridge from here to there. Twenty-two years of indigenous autonomy in post-modern Chiapas is a truly stunning achievement.† The best of the European revolutionary tradition can scarcely point to anything like this in living memory. It's not perfect, but I'll take a flawed reality that I can hold in my hands over a perfect ideal that I can never touch, every time.

* According to the reports of Paul Z. Simons in *Modern Slavery,* the YPG/YPJ (People's Protection Units/Women's Protection Units) have taken a similar position in the liberated territories of Rojava.

† See the works of James C. Scott for other examples in the post-modern world, as well as David Graeber's writings on Madagascar. For some overlooked examples from American history, see the story of Maroon communities in the Great Dismal Swamp in *The Real Resistance to Slavery in North America* by Russell Maroon Shoats, as well as the story of Henry Berry Lowry and the Swamp Bandits in *Dixie Be Damned* by Neal Shirley and Saralee Stafford.

So far, so good, but there's no denying that things haven't gone very well in Mexico for the past decade. The Zapatista enclaves remain, but elsewhere everything has gone from bad to worse. The Mexican state has drawn a line in the sand. They've lost control of part of Chiapas, but they'd rather set their own house on fire than risk losing control of the rest of it. The September 2014 kidnapping and murder of 43 students from the Ayotzinapa Rural Teacher's College in Iguala, Guerrero‡ sent a clear message that *La Otra Campaña* is finished, that indigenous autonomy will not be allowed to spread to other parts of Mexico, and that there is nothing that the Zapatistas can do about it anymore. What happened?

I'll defer to Mexicans more directly involved in this, but as an American participating in the movement, here's my take: it comes down to guns. At the moment, autonomous zones exist only where tolerated (as in Chiapas) or fiercely defended (as in Rojava). Spaces of autonomy that are not tolerated and cannot defend themselves will be wiped off the face of the earth. It gives me no joy to say this.

Armed self-defense can turn into war very quickly. War is costly—in blood and treasure. Weapons and ammunition don't come cheaply and have to come from some source. So armed struggle almost always demands state support. This is obviously

‡ The students went missing on September 26, after commandeering several buses to travel to Mexico City to observe the anniversary of the 1968 Tlatelolco Massacre. Local police detained them during the journey; none of the students were ever seen alive again. The official investigation concluded that once the students were in police custody, they were handed over to local cartel operatives and killed. Other reports state that the Mexican army was directly involved in the murders. The mass disappearance marked arguably the biggest crisis Mexican President Enrique Peña Nieto had yet faced in his administration. The incident drew worldwide attention and triggered sustained protests, particularly in Guerrero and Mexico City. The case resonated so strongly because it highlighted the level of collusion organized crime had reached with local governments, police agencies, and the military. See *The Disappeared* by John Gibler.

a conundrum. Why would any state want to preserve spaces of autonomy? Generally, they don't.

Fine, but this generally means that when revolution turns into war, autonomy is the first casualty. Central to the Zapatista's breakthrough was their understanding that war is not won on the battlefield alone—the driving force of the revolution is not to be found in armed conflict but in a better way of life. Unfortunately, the state always seems to have an ace in the hole.

Against all odds, the Zapatistas remain unvanquished. Their ongoing revolution has been an inspiration to millions of people worldwide for an entire generation, myself included. But the path to another world that they tried to open to us all has been submerged in an ocean of blood.

There is no easy solution to this dilemma. These same dynamics turned Syria into a living hell, as various participants in the civil war escalated the level of violence until they had stripped themselves of their humanity and converted each other into symmetrical killing machines. The revolutionaries in Rojava are walking a razor's edge, forced to balance the danger of being co-opted by the American government tomorrow against that of being annihilated by ISIS today. The Zapatistas have been juggling these machetes for over twenty years.

All I can say is that it's generally undesirable for revolution to turn into war, that nonetheless sometimes it will, and that when it does both will be won or lost together. It won't be possible to win the war by abandoning the revolution, or to advance the revolution while ignoring the war. I've seen the same patterns recur in history, current events, and my own experiences.

In 2010 and 2011, I spent some time working with Triqui people from the municipality of San Juan Copala in Oaxaca. Triquis there had taken part in the 2006 uprising in Oaxaca, and in January 2007 the municipality declared autonomy along the lines of the Zapatista model. By November 2009, paramilitaries aligned with the state government had placed the entire community under siege, cutting off access to water, food, medical services, and electricity. Gunmen stationed in the hills surrounding the town were shooting at anything that moved. Numerous people were killed.[*]

On April 27, 2010, a small group of outside supporters, also veterans of the 2006 uprising, attempted to break the siege with a caravan of several vehicles full of food, water, and medical supplies. Paramilitaries ambushed the caravan outside of Copala, shooting and killing two participants: Alberta "Bety" Cariño Trujillo (a widely-respected Mixteca and the director of an indigenous organization named CACTUS) and Jyri Jaakkola (a Finnish solidarity worker who was well-integrated into the Oaxacan social struggle). The survivors escaped into the mountains, several wounded, emerging alive days later and many miles away after having sent out gripping videos of the ordeal over their cellphones. The story briefly made American news; the outcry in Mexico was tremendous.

I think it's fair to say that the story was especially compelling to many people because of who died. In Bety's case, Triquis and Mixtecas have a very long and contentious history. In the American context, it might be like if a Hopi woman was killed while attempting to stop the relocation of Navajo (Diné) elders on Black Mesa,[†] or if an Ojibwe woman was killed while bringing supplies to Lakota water protectors at Standing Rock.[‡] And Jyri was *Finnish*. It was not lost on anyone that he had come from halfway across the world to risk his life for indigenous autonomy.

"Many people thought it was strange that he was involved," one of the survivors of the first caravan told me once. "It wasn't.

[*] All this met with profound disinterest from most of Mexican society, including the Mexican left. Triquis are one of the more marginalized indigenous groups in Mexico; they are constantly depicted as genetically unreasonable and violent. Picture an uninformed American talking about the Middle East: "They're always killing each other." Well, why might that be?

[†] See Black Mesa Indigenous Support at supportblackmesa.org for more on this.
[‡] Check the Red Warrior Camp Facebook page for more on the resistance to the Dakota Access Pipeline on the Standing Rock Indian Reservation in North Dakota.

Jyri knew exactly what he was getting into. He was one of us, and his death was a terrible loss." Copala is the only campaign that I've ever been involved with in which I would regularly see indigenous people carrying around pictures of a martyred white solidarity worker, rather than the other way around. Bety and Jyri's names will be tied together as long as either of them are remembered.

In June 2010, a much larger caravan was organized to break the siege, this time comprised of numerous buses and dump trucks full of hundreds of people and supplies from all over Mexico. I was there, too. Even by my standards, this was a hair-raising experience. The caravan was repeatedly held up by police as it approached Copala, and shadowed by groups of masked gunmen posted on the hills above the road. It's impossible to say if they were police, military, paramilitary, or some combination of the three. Shortly before nightfall, several miles outside the town, the uniformed police announced that they wouldn't guarantee our security, and they all left.

This was a do or die moment. It was very hard to say what would happen next. As participants in the caravan, we had agreed to defer ultimate decision-making power to a core group of Triquis from San Juan Copala. This leadership had agreed to take input from all participants into consideration. Leadership was faced with a very difficult choice. They decided to turn back.

This caused a complete uproar. People were screaming at each other in the middle of the road and trying to decide what to do. The reader may remember the Gaza Freedom Flotilla of May 31, 2010, when nine humanitarian aid workers were killed by the Israeli military while attempting to break the blockade of the Gaza Strip. That occurred just a matter of days before our caravan. The Triqui leadership, to paraphrase, said: "Palestine is known throughout the world. They just killed those people in cold blood, and nothing happened. We're a small indigenous group. Nobody knows about us anywhere. The paramilitaries have already shown that they'll kill people, and the government won't do·anything about it. We know them well; this is too dangerous. If we don't turn back, some of you are going to die.

We already have the deaths of two outsiders on our consciences. We don't want any more."

Many participants said in turn: "This is your only chance. You'll never have this much momentum again. What did you call us here for if you didn't think you could call their bluff? If you turn back now, the government will take it as a sign of weakness, and they will destroy you within a few months. It will be a setback for indigenous autonomy everywhere. This is bigger than you, it's bigger than any of us. If they kill us, there's at least some chance that Mexico will explode." Leadership deliberated one more time, and turned us back. Within a few months, the paramilitaries burned out the last inhabitants of the autonomous municipality, culminating in a final offensive of killings and rapes in September 2010. As of 2016, displaced people from Copala are still camped out in the Zócalo in the city of Oaxaca. They have never been able to return home.

In the years since, I've spoken with several of the people who had to make this decision. I also learned that one of them had subsequently migrated through the Arivaca corridor in 2011, picking up water that we had set out along the way. I can see that the retreat still weighs heavy on them. It may have been where *La Otra Campaña* died; it may have saved my life. Nobody can say; I don't know myself. I'm afraid both statements may be correct. I consented to defer to those people and I respect the decision that they made.

In the aftermath of the second caravan, I would hear conversations like this: "They've left you two choices: surrender or war." The response would be: "The paramilitaries are financed by the state government. We are poor people, financed by nobody. It's all well and good to talk about armed struggle. If we went to war, how would we afford guns and ammunition, and where would we get them? Are *you* going to supply them? We would lose."

The siege of San Juan Copala taught me a hard lesson: unarmed resistance is suicide in the face of a ruthless enough foe, but armed struggle without state support may be suicide as well. Writing in 1943, George Orwell suggested that this was why fascism triumphed in the Spanish Civil War as well. In *Looking*

Back on the Spanish War, he argues that the outcome of the war was settled in London, Washington, and Paris when the West declined to arm the revolutionary militias.

In military terms, I'm afraid Orwell was right. When unarmed resistance turns into armed conflict, military considerations cannot be ignored or wished away. So is it better to seek state support in hopes of winning, or to not do so and almost certainly lose? Every situation is different. I honestly don't know.

Fortunately, there's another way to tell this story. In revolutionary terms, we can agree with Orwell that the outcome of the struggle in Spain was indeed determined in Paris and Washington and London—and Moscow and Marrakesh and Algiers—but not by the authorities. It was determined by the common people when they chose not to rise up and extend the revolution from Spain to the rest of the world.[*] We might never be able to count on heads of state, but we can hope that the people *they* count on will sometimes refuse to carry out their orders.

As long as revolt is spreading and the authorities do not know who will be the next to break ranks, the ordinary rules of war do not apply. In this situation, a drastically under-equipped populace can outmaneuver a world-class military. This is precisely what occurred in France in 1848, in Russia in 1917, and in Egypt in 2011. In each case, it was only afterwards, when a new configuration of authorities was established—supposedly to complete and fulfill the revolution—that the movement was crushed.

On March 18, 1871, French soldiers refused to obey an order to fire on women and workers. That single refusal gave birth to the Paris Commune, one of the most famous revolutionary autonomous zones in history, and it was nearly enough to topple the entire government of France. For a few days, the whole country trembled on the brink of revolution as everyone waited to see whether other soldiers would desert, other cities rise up. But the Commune was defeated from the moment that it started firing back on the army that was sent to force it out of Paris. Until

[*] Orwell is sympathetic to this position in *Homage to Catalonia,* written in 1938 a few months after he served on the Spanish front.

that point, the government was terrified that the rest of the military would revolt, too; but once ordinary soldiers regarded the Commune as a military enemy, it was just a war again, and the woefully outnumbered and underequipped Communards were bound to lose.

This illustrates the difference between war and revolution. I think the Zapatistas understood this: they recognized that they needed enough firepower to repel the Mexican government, but that the threat that their revolt might become contagious was the most powerful weapon in their arsenal.

To put this all together, the short-term survival of autonomous territories often depends on physical superiority over a completely ruthless foe, which unfortunately demands an arms supply and arms suppliers. I've seen this with my own eyes. Mid-term survival likely depends on revolutionary momentum spreading far enough to keep the place from being encircled, embargoed, and economically choked into submission, and long-term survival ultimately implies some kind of global revolutionary transformation. The faster all this takes place, the less bloody it is likely to be.

For what it's worth, the defeat at Copala does seem to have informed later struggles such as the ones in Santa María Ostula and Cherán, both in Michoacán. The Nahua community of Ostula set a precedent in the region when it rose up in arms to protect its land from resource extraction carried out by local cartels affiliated with the state government, namely iron mining and the illegal logging of the endangered sangualica tree.[†] The Purepecha community of Cheran also rose up in arms in 2011 to defend its communal forests from logging operations affiliated with the state government and local cartels.[‡] Both communities have organized *rondas communitarias* (community militias) to defend themselves from attack. I don't know where the money or weapons come from in Ostula or Cherán, but I'm willing to bet that part of the explanation for the success of the *rondas* and

† See the *Ostula Manifesto,* enacted in June 2009.
‡ See the 2013 documentary *Guarda Bosques (Forest Keepers)* by Manovuelta.

the expansion of indigenous autonomy in Michoacán is that this question has been answered there somehow.

Cherán and Ostula committed themselves to collective armed self-defense, while Copala did not. Copala was annihilated. People who fed me, told me stories, advocated for my wellbeing, and stood by my side during the second caravan were left widowed, orphaned, homeless, in prison, living in exile, and dead. Thus far, Cherán and Ostula remain standing. This is probably not a coincidence.

"The price of freedom is death."

– Malcolm X

Solidarity

I'll assume for the moment that the reader is a citizen of the global north, like myself, and at least vaguely uneasy about the direction things are headed. If global revolutionary transformation is indeed necessary to avert chaos and war on a planetary scale—or at least, to prevent them from becoming worse than they are already sure to be*—then how do we participate?

Solidarity work is certainly one entry point. Since the end of World War II, many sober critics of capitalism have concluded that the probability of revolution in the global north is zero, and that it makes more sense to focus attention elsewhere. They seem to have been mostly right about that. Furthermore, starting from the assumption that all lives have equal and inherent value, there's no denying that the majority of the people suffering the most at the moment don't hail from the global north, and that it makes sense to prioritize the worst suffering first. There are some downsides to this approach, though, and I think I've seen all of them.

Solidarity workers are faced with an apparent conflict of interest. Like most other people, we are subject to global capitalism. We too face an uncertain future. We feel a responsibility to intervene when people are systematically mistreated in our name, against our will, and with our tax dollars. However, it appears that intervening often makes our own lives more precarious and unstable, not less. While most everyone else looks to reduce the degree of precarity they experience (for instance, by migrating), we appear to be seeking it out.

There's only one path out of this state of cognitive dissonance: to recognize how our own wellbeing is tied to the wellbeing

---

* Regarding climate change, it looks like that ship has sailed, but we can still exert some influence on how rapidly we accelerate towards the abyss. If nothing else, taking action puts us in touch with our agency and makes for an interesting life. For now, some of us are able to opt out of actively participating in these conflicts, but doing so just means that more assertive people will shape the context we live in. We won't get the world we deserve; we'll get the world we have the leverage to bring about. For further exploration of this line of thinking, see *Desert*, published anonymously in England in 2011.

of others. The people working in solidarity with migrants and refugees in Greece are demonstrating this clearly.* Greece could be expelled from the European Union at any moment, or leave of its own accord. Greek solidarity workers may soon find themselves without EU citizenship, outside of the border. If Greeks don't care about Syrians today, who will care about Greeks tomorrow?

This is where the privilege politics that are so prevalent in the American activist milieu fall fatally short. People who are motivated by guilt and shame rather than by love and rage will eventually disengage; people who are not fighting for their own lives will eventually give up. Always.†

We went deep into the mountains, deeper than we had ever gone before. We thought that there was traffic going through there, but the area was so hard to reach that we had never been able to find out for sure. These were different mountains, and we didn't know them very well.

We reached the trail early in the morning of the second day. Within five minutes, we ran into a migrant who was walking by himself. He looked tired but was in pretty good shape. He asked us how far he had to go. I had to tell him that I didn't really know. We gave him food and water. He went on by himself, and we kept going.

The trail was worse than any I had ever seen, and I had seen plenty of bad ones. It crossed five large canyons, dropping and climbing about two thousand feet each time. There were signs of heavy use. We found a shrine on a ridge between two of these canyons, carefully tended with little grottos for different saints. We made slow progress, burned through most of our water by late afternoon, and it became clear that we could not make it back out to be picked up before dark. We decided to drop down one more time and find somewhere to sleep.

* The Lesvos Solidarity camp in Mytilene, Lesvos is one example. See lesvossolidarity.org for more information.

† See "Lines in the Sand" by Peter Gelderloos and "Another Word For White Ally Is Coward" by Anti-State STL.

As we approached the bottom, we rounded a corner in the canyon near a large cave. My companion and I stopped abruptly. "Oh fuck," he said. "That's fucked up. Cut that down." Someone had used quite a bit of rope to carefully hang a woman's bra and shorts from a tree in front of the cave at about the position where they would be located if there was a real person standing there. I could only guess that these clothes had belonged to someone who had been raped there, and that they had been left as a trophy or memento to the event by the person who had done it. I had heard reports and found evidence of this practice in other places before. I cut them down.

It was almost dark. We reached the bottom, backed into a side canyon, and slept inside a thick tangle of catclaw. One of my companions woke us up in the middle of the night, screaming at nothing.

The next day was far hotter than the one before. I had not seen this coming, as it was still early in the year. We had very little water left, and two more ridges to cross. By the time we climbed to the top of the last ridge I was starting to get sick. I felt unusually weak, and my heart was beating abnormally and alarmingly fast. I lay down under a little tree to try to get out of the sun. I said something to one of my companions. They did not respond because they were a large rock.

"I'm sorry," I said, when I found them again. "I don't feel good. Please keep an eye on me." I walked the last miles down to the car in a daze without anything to drink. I kept thinking about the Gatorade that I had given the migrant, wondering if he would be OK and thinking that I wouldn't mind finding a gallon of water on the trail right about now. I thought about how I would feel if I didn't have a phone in my pocket, a GPS around my neck, and friends by my side. There seemed to be bones everywhere: deer, coyote, rabbit, skunk, cattle.

"Now we walk through the valley of the shadow of death," one of my companions said. I had been working in the desert for years and was in excellent shape. It is amazing how fast anyone can deteriorate in the sun without water to drink.

Myself, I came to the desert dead broke and not that young anymore, a late Generation X castoff of the anti-globalization movement. Having ridden that wave from the very beginning to the bitter end, I washed up in Tucson with no evident prospect of employment and a murky work history, but an extensive résumé in rioting. I couldn't figure out anything better to do. Much of the rest of the volunteer base were early Millennials who had gone into a mountain of debt only to find that their degrees didn't guarantee them a place in the middle class at all.

No More Deaths took us in and said: "We can't pay you, but we'll take care of you. Here's a phone, here are the keys to the trucks, here's money for gas, here's the number of a lawyer if you end up in trouble, here's the number of a doctor if you get sick or hurt. You can live out here. Here's something that you can do; here's something that you can be proud of. We trust you; you just have to do the work." Don't underestimate the effect that this can have. I was used to coming up with all of this on my own; this little safety net made me feel like I was invincible.* It worked for a long time. I left the desert seven years older, in basically the same position as when I arrived.

I'm not conflating my experiences with those of migrants and refugees. I spent a lot of time in their company, however, and I came to realize that we were looking for a lot of the same things. In a world that seemed to have no place for us, we were desperate to be told: "You are not expendable; you have something to offer; you can be of use. You are wanted; you are respected; you are loved. What you do matters; your actions make a difference; your life means something. Here's something you can do; here's something you can be proud of; here's something bigger than yourself." This is called dignity. People hunger for it; its absence gnaws at them like phantom pain from an amputated limb.

* Working in the desert taught me a lot about how resilient projects can be when they draw on multi-generational depth. When people of all ages bring different resources to the table, the whole is suddenly much greater than the sum of its parts.

> "I am also discovering a degree of strength and of basic ability for humans to remain human in the direst of circumstances—which I also haven't seen before. I think the word is dignity. I wish you could meet these people. Maybe, hopefully, someday you will."

> – Rachel Corrie, writing to her mother, February 28th, 2003

Undocumented and displaced people don't need it any less than the rest of us; they need it even more. Many times I heard things like, "I wish I could just stay here and work with you guys; I wish I could go out with you to leave water in the desert; I wish I could do something for my people." Especially from Central American teenagers with no place to go.

It is a perversion of dignity that all of these cynical paymasters offer us instead: a gun, a few dollars, a license to kill, a paycheck, a mortgage, a numb resignation to something that we know is wrong. Nihilism fills us up with empty calories, but it's not strong food. It's one thing to hold a weapon in your hands; it's quite another to do so guided by great feelings of love. Che Guevara was right about this.

When people find both a purpose and the means to actualize it, they seem to acquire superhuman powers. It's as though they can walk through walls and bullets pass right through them. That's how people make it through the border and home to their families. It's why Harriet Tubman never lost a passenger and Crazy Horse never lost a battle;* it's why ISIS crested and then was broken on the rock of Kobanê.† "Hope with a trigger," said the *Second Declaration of the Lacandón Jungle* in June 1994. "Arms with a compass," they might have added.

And it's why in all those years of desert aid work, we never gave up.‡

Luther walked into camp during the winter of 2011. Like many other people, he was frozen, dehydrated, and half-starved. Unlike many other people, he also had worms, and he walked on four legs. Luther is a tomcat: the greatest cat who ever lived.

When Luther first arrived, I was apprehensive. I was not convinced that it was a good idea to add another creature to our long list of concerns. Weeks passed, however, and no one could find him another home.

Around this time, a woman from Oaxaca arrived at camp. It was cold and raining. She was sitting in the medical tent, soaked to the skin, shivering, crying, and clearly distraught. I could see that she was not convinced that she could trust us.

All of a sudden, Luther barged into the tent, jumped into her lap, and began kneading her legs enthusiastically while purring like an outboard motor. The change in her demeanor was stunning. She looked like a huge weight had been thrown off her shoulders.

"*Oh… qué lindo… qué cariñoso el gato…*"

I looked at Luther in amazement as he went about his work. "Maybe you *do* have a place here," I remember thinking.

---

* Research the Combahee River Raid and the Battle of the Greasy Grass, June 2, 1863 and June 25-26, 1876 respectively, for the high points of the careers of Harriet Tubman and Crazy Horse and arguably the two greatest direct actions in American history. See *Jailbreak Out Of History* by Butch Lee.

† See *Understanding the Kurdish Resistance,* published by CrimethInc. in 2015.
‡ "We are an army of dreamers, and that's why we're invincible." -Subcommandante Marcos

Luther had found his home, and before long, he looked like a miniature jaguar—with sleek black fur, rippling sinewy muscles, and paws like catcher's mitts. I firmly believe that he came to understand that he has a specific role at camp, and that doing his duties is what earns him his supper. His job is to make the people feel better. Time and again I saw him demonstrate an uncanny ability to pull both migrants and volunteers back from the brink of despair, at precisely the moment they felt weakest and most vulnerable. He certainly did this for me on many occasions.

I hesitate to say this, but I think that there is also something about Luther's dark and handsome masculine energy that can be especially comforting to some women. I once spent the better part of a week at camp with three Guatemalan women who would pass the time making up uproarious and occasionally ribald tales of Luther's prowess.

"Oh, Luther, he has *three women* here at camp who are all in love with him, but that is not enough for him. He must go out into the night and leave us here alone, awaiting his return. However will we manage without him? Whatever will we do?"

Luther is not only a lover, though. He is also a fighter. He has another job to do. He battles rattlesnakes.

Personally, I like rattlesnakes. They are reasonable creatures. They are not generally aggressive. We moved into their home, not the other way around. They can be dangerous, though. Once, a migrant got bitten in the medical tent. It's not good to have rattlesnakes inside of a humanitarian aid camp.

Luther patrols his domain vigilantly, and he goes berserk whenever he finds rattlesnakes inside of it. He hisses and screams until somebody notices, and usually we are able to capture the snake and relocate it away from camp. Sometimes, he tries to fight them on his own. This is a risky business. Once, he got bitten in the face. It swelled up like a grapefruit, but he pulled through.

Luther is known far and wide, from Tacoma to Tegucigalpa. One time, a teenager from northern Sonora walked into camp, looking for water and painkillers for his group, looking himself like a desperate, hunted, and famished wolf. Luther was sitting on the table.

"*¡Lucer!*" the young man said, with a huge smile breaking across his weather-beaten face. He scooped him into his arms and began vigorously rubbing his furry head. "*¡A la verga, güey!*" he added, a phrase so thoroughly obscene that I refuse to translate it. For a second, he looked like a normal teenager rather than a despised beast of no nation.

Desert aid work took a major leap forward when Luther walked into camp. He became our avatar, our collective responsibility, and the unifying mythos of our work. No other member of No More Deaths has put in as much time at camp. It's not even close.

When the great book of names is written—that honors the memory of the human and non-human animals who have contributed to the collective liberation of all humanity and of all sentient beings—the name of Luther the Tomcat will be inscribed in its pages.

Home

We are products of our environment, and I know mine well. There are some good things about American culture; it is also characterized by a strong tendency toward individualism and exceptionalism. Many undocumented people have tried to explain to me how difficult this is to get used to. It can be difficult for those of us who grew up in it to see it at all. To identify this is not self-loathing or mere anti-Americanism—it's a reality check. People from other places have a responsibility to examine themselves as well.

As Americans, we are told to think of ourselves as rugged individuals in a land of meritocracy and equal opportunity. We feel like we should be able to pull ourselves up by our own bootstraps, and we feel like failures if we can't. We take everything personally, can't see structure, and won't pool our resources. We're a proud people, all right; we can take care of ourselves— from rags to riches, from pawns to kings. These habits make us spectacularly easy to control. We run ourselves ragged to pay

"Me
We"

*– Muhammad Ali, 1974,
the shortest poem ever written*

for food, clothing, shelter, health care, and transportation on an individual basis. We run frantically in place on our personal hamster wheels alone. As soon as we have children, there's no evident way to do anything else. It's no wonder our only apparent alternative is in youth culture; there's really no way to stay in the game as an adult.

As Americans, we are also told that we live in a city on a hill, separate and exempt from the forces affecting the rest of the world. We are told that our history is inherently different from the history of other places, that we have a unique mission to transform the world, and that this history and mission make us superior to other people. We don't have to understand anything about what is going on in the rest of the world—it doesn't concern us. Yet at the same time, we don't know how to mind our own business; we are hell-bent on transforming the whole world in our image. This combination of selfishness, ignorance, and arrogance can be hard for many other people to swallow.

The US government's drunken piracy in Iraq may have been the final nail in the coffin. It won't be possible to see the world this way much longer without literally burying our heads in the sand. An army of one is easily surrounded. All of these tendencies will prove more and more maladaptive in the years to come; we'll break these habits or these habits will break us. It won't be easy, but the difference between hard and impossible is a thousand miles wide. We can do it.

This unbalanced worldview is not unique to my culture. Its roots are in the dis-integration of the self from the other, of the individual from the collective, of the spiritual from the physical, of one family of humans from another, and of humanity from the rest of the web of life. These divides are successfully bridged nowhere in post-modern civilization. Every place is different, but it's out of balance everywhere. It's no wonder that we find ourselves lost in a labyrinth, each of us isolated inside a concentric set of rings, each border more heavily fortified than the last. It's driving us crazy. We're not meant to go it alone.

The Lakota prayer *Mitákuye Oyás'iŋ* (All My Relations; All Are Related) is not a metaphor but a precise description of reality. If we look back far enough, every human being on the planet shares common ancestry; if we look back further, so does every living thing; and ultimately, everything in existence shares common origins in the Big Bang. Every time people begin to place themselves outside the web of life, they end up in the same position: guarding the walls of a collapsing empire, as their forsaken cousins gather to pull down their temples and tear the flesh from their bones. The defenders of segregation are leading us down a path to certain destruction. They abandoned their families; it's time for us to find our way back home. There is a light to guide us through the desert: the faithful northern star.

For anarchy: the transformative interplay between chaos and order,

an ex-desert-aid-worker
North America
2011, 2016

The border divides the whole world into gated communities and prisons, one within the other in concentric circles of privilege and control. At one end of the continuum, there are billionaires who can fly anywhere in private jets; at the other end, inmates in solitary confinement. As long as there is a border between you and those less fortunate than you, you can be sure there will be a border above you, too, keeping you from the things you need.

And who will tear down that second border with you, if not the people separated from you by the first?

In memory of the thirteen people
who died on my bus in Mexico:
you could have been me;
I could have been you.
Rest in peace.